OF REVOLUTION

Clare Doyle

Month of Revolution
by Clare Doyle

First Edition May 1988

ISBN No 1 870958 02 0

Published by Fortress Books, PO Box 141,
London E2 ORL
Typeset and Produced by Eastway Offset Ltd (TU)
3/13 Hepscott Road, London E9 5HB (01-533-3311)

Single Copies available from Fortress Books

Trade Distribution: Central Books, 14 The
Leathermarket, London SE1 3ER

Produced with the invaluable assistance of
comrades of the *Militant*. (C.D)

Cover design by Richard Evans

Fortress Books is a socialist publishing house. We encourage readers of our works to actively participate in the struggle for socialism. If you would like to receive more information about the ideas and events in this book, or have any comments and suggestions, you are welcome to contact the author via Fortress Books, PO Box 141, London E2 ORL

Contents

'Revolutions are festivals of the oppressed and the exploited. At no other time are the mass of the people in a position to come forward so actively as creators of a new social order, as at a time of revolution. At such times the people are capable of performing miracles, if judged by the limited, philistine yardstick of gradualist progress. But it is essential that leaders of the revolutionary parties, too, should advance their aims more comprehensively and boldly at such a time, so that their slogans shall always be in advance of the revolutionary initiative of the masses, serve as a beacon, reveal to them our democratic and socialist ideal in all its magnitude and splendour, and show them the shortest and most direct route to complete, absolute, and decisive victory.'

Lenin. (*Two Tactics of Social Democracy in the Democratic Revolution*) 1905

A Revolution in the Making

THE 'MAY EVENTS' of France 1968 constituted the greatest general strike in history. It erupted like an exploding volcano. The shock waves reached every corner of the world. The aftereffects will never truly subside. At its height, ten million workers were on strike. They occupied their workplaces, hoisted the red flag and set up committees. They sang the *Internationale* and hotly debated how to take control of their lives. Every layer in society was swept along by the tidal wave which flowed towards a new form of society—a break with the past and a flowering of human talent. Few saw the approach of this great movement; millions felt its effects, and ruling classes everywhere trembled at what the consequences might be.

The titanic clash of class forces apparently came like a bolt from the blue. World capitalism was basking in the sunshine of an unprecedented post-war boom, which many commentators believed was unending. Even some claiming to be 'Marxists' decided that capitalism had found a way of 'amortising' (solving) its crises!

France's special 'chromium-plated' boom had started late with the coming to power of General Charles de Gaulle in 1958. By 1968 it was providing a healthy 5 per cent rate of growth and gaining ground for French goods on the world market. 'All was for the best in the best of all possible worlds', as Voltaire's character Pangloss liked to believe!

But none of the basic contradictions and conflicts of capitalist society had been eliminated. On the contrary, they had been aggravated and exacerbated, and would inevitably lead to new crises and new explosions in the class struggle. Just as, nearly twenty years later, it was only the Marxists around the *Militant* who predicted the world stock market crash of 1987 and the convulsions which followed, it was only they who understood the processes taking place in 1968. They were adamant that explosive changes were ahead, and that the socialist revolution would re-emerge in Europe with a vengeance.

The 'Communist' Party in France continued to peddle the line, inherited from the pre-war leader Maurice Thorez, that revolution was impossible in France as long as living standards in Russia remained lower than those of Western Europe! The false perspectives of other so-called Marxists were summed up in an article by the French 'theoretician' André Gorz, in the January 1968 *Socialist Register*:'In the forseeable future, there will be no crisis of European capitalism so dramatic as to drive the mass of workers to revolutionary general strikes.'

The PCI (International Communist Party) whose youth organisation, the JCR, was already heavily involved in the student struggles in France, echoed these ideas. Claiming to stand on the ideas of Trotsky, in reality they had completely abandoned them. At a meeting in London only weeks before the outbreak of the general strike, they claimed that such a development would not be possible within the next twenty years! Workers in the metropolitan cities were 'defeated' and 'on the retreat', they declared.

They had turned their backs on the working class of Europe and looked elsewhere for their 'revolution'. They concentrated on students everywhere and uncritically sang the praises of the Stalinist-leaning leaders of the colonial revolutions of Cuba, Algeria and Vietnam (which they said were analogous to the Russian revolution of 1917).

The full impact—the scale, the scope, the sweep – of the revolutionary movement which took place in France, still astonished even those who were expecting a movement of the working class in the advanced capitalist countries. It gave a glimpse of the revolutionary past of France and a taste of what is to come–not only in France, but throughout Europe and indeed the world.

It was not just *Militant* in May and June 1968 that recognised a new French revolution in the making. The French general Beaufre declared: 'The times we live in are undoubtedly those of the birth of a revolution of which it is impossible to predict the course of events.'

As always, the serious strategists of capital came to the same conclusions as the Marxists, although from the opposite standpoint. The *Financial Times* on 22 May, 1968, reflected the terror of the world's bourgeoisie at the prospects:

> When Louis Philippe was driven from his throne in 1848, after a few brisk days of rioting in Paris and took refuge in London, there were revolutions all over Europe. Italy, West Germany, Belgium and Spain are in trouble enough without the 'Mother of Revolutions' once again setting a bad example.

The London *Evening Standard* declared on 29 May: 'The situation today can be summed up in a few words: it is a revolutionary situation of an almost text-book kind.' *The Economist* (1 June) was drawing the same conclusion, although only a week earlier it had spoken of France not being a revolutionary country!

Once the revolutionary storm had subsided and the commentators had recovered their balance, their tune changed. The 'May Events' were declared 'exceptional', an 'aberration', an 'episode'–unforgettable but nevertheless an 'episode'. French society had never really been threatened, they insisted. But such a mighty movement could not be

The 'Social Peace' of the boom was shattered.

buried with declarations. Twenty years later the questions remain: Could it happen again? Could it happen in any other country? Could it happen in *every* other country?

That a general strike of such proportions could take place in an industrialised capitalist society is a constant nightmare not only for the French ruling class but for many others besides. As world recession approaches, the 'spectre of '68' looms larger than ever.

By 1968 there had been a prolonged post-war boom. It had provided a breathing space for workers. The wounds of past defeats and disappointments were healed over. Their organisations grew in numbers and cohesion. The employers, making vast profits, seemed more favourably disposed to accede to workers' demands. Class relations were apparently softened. In this climate, the ideas of reformism could gain ground. The illusion that capitalism could provide for workers' needs little-by-little led the leaders of the workers' organisations to abandon the idea that socialism was necessary.

The analysis of the so-called Trotskyist theoreticians was the other side of the same coin. They, along with numerous academics, 'discovered' another phenomenon that they claimed would prevent workers moving towards socialism–the existence of the 'strong state'. In France this was personified in the figure of Charles de Gaulle. He had come to power in 1958, posing as the 'saviour of the nation' in a situation of crisis in the economy, with a 'mission' to defeat the liberation war for Algerian independence.

A Strong State?

Engels, Marx's collaborator, explained how, at certain stages of the class struggle, the state rises above society and appears, more than usual,to be detached from the interests of either of the main contending forces. Despite the appearance of balancing between the classes, the state ultimately reflects the interests of the economically dominant class, in the case of de Gaulle, the French capitalists.

De Gaulle himself claimed that he represented a 'third way–between capitalism and communism'. He did nothing of the sort! He had saved France for capitalism but to do so he had been forced to lean on other classes in society. He even had to take measures that a section of the capitalists and the petty bourgeois found distasteful–particularly those bitterly opposed to the abandonment of the French colony in Algeria. He also introduced measures of state interference in the otherwise unfettered rule of capital that benefited big business but squeezed the petty bourgeois and especially small businesses. Furthermore, he exercised extraordinary censorship of the media, partially restricting the right even of these layers to debate, discuss and criticise.

A special form of personal power was in operation. De Gaulle had declared on becoming President: 'I belong to everyone and everyone belongs to me.' He proceeded to disregard parliament, preferring to rule by decree, tempered with the plebiscite–a referendum of 'the people'.

Lacking a firm base of social support, a bonapartist state relies ultimately on the 'sword'–the armed bodies of men. De Gaulle's bonapartism was a most limited, parliamentary type when compared to the naked police dictatorships that existed in many parts of the world. Nevertheless, it was a brutal regime whose natural reaction at times of crisis was 'strike first and consider afterwards'. It did not work against protesting students. It was even less likely to succeed against the powerful new generation of French workers whose organisations were still intact.

To keep order in the France of de Gaulle, there were more members of the forces of the state per head of the population than in almost any other advanced capitalist country in the world. But even this powerful state machine crumbled at the first real test of its mettle, confounding the theories of all those who had abandoned the working class.

A revolutionary situation like that which developed in France in May 1968 can make 20 years seem like one day and as Marx put it, 'days come in which 20 years are concentrated'. A revolutionary situation cannot by its very nature last indefinitely, but only for days, weeks, or at most months. In Russia it lasted as long as perhaps three months. There are

The 'Strong State' in action. Act first—consider afterwards!

different stages in the development of events during a revolution but never, as the 'Communist' Parties still try to maintain, can the struggle for democracy be separated as a different 'stage' from the struggle for socialism. De Gaulle's access to power had shown how fragile democracy can be in a capitalist society. Only if the reins of the economy are taken over by the working class can such a thing as socialist democracy be established. The events of France 1968 showed that this idea was far from utopian. Every layer of society seemed to be convinced in action that there was a more practical, just and humane way of organising things than that dictated by capitalism. The events also demonstrated conclusively that the task of the socialist revolution can be carried out by no other class than the working class itself. In France 1968, given the great power of the working class and the support of the middle classes, the socialist revolution could have been carried through peacefully and in a matter of days.

Students take to the Streets

THE WAY IN which events unfolded in 1968 seemed at first sight to confirm the claims of students throughout the world that they could 'detonate' revolution. No doubt the governments of a number of countries were beginning to tremble at such a prospect! The world was experiencing an unprecedented wave of student unrest–Poland, Italy, Spain, Germany, Britain and America. Some of these struggles had reached a higher pitch than in France.

In Spain the students fought the dictator Franco. In the United States, students were to the fore in the movement against the Vietnam war and in the black consciousness and civil rights movement in the South. In Northern Ireland, students were involved in an upsurge of struggle against anti-Catholic discrimination. Intellectuals, students and sections of the workers in Czechoslovakia were being drawn into a profound political ferment known as the 'Prague Spring'.

Big battles had erupted in all the major university towns of Germany. An attempt was even made on the life of the student leader Rudi Dutschke. In Britain as elsewhere students were on the march in their tens of thousands against the American war in Vietnam. Although the student struggles were symptomatic of deeper social conflicts, nowhere else other than in France did they spark off a general strike of workers, let alone one that could have brought to an end the rule of capital.

What is the explanation? It lies not in any superior methods adopted by the French students, but in the coming together of all the political and social preconditions for revolution–the combustible material. The bonapartism of de Gaulle acted as an additional and aggravating 'detonator'.

French students had been involved in big movements against the Algerian war in the early 1960s. They had demonstrated as vociferously as any in support of the struggle in Vietnam for independence. This was a particularly potent issue because it revived the memories of France's inglorious attempt to hold on to its former colony of Indo-China. It was after France's catastrophic defeat at Dien Bien Phu that US imperialism had assumed domination of South Vietnam.

In early 1968 it was protests against a restrictive education system and archaic rules which erupted into open clashes on the campuses. With the renowned subtlety of a frightened bureaucracy, the authorities called in the forces of the state. On a number of occasions, police 'put down' the troubles. At the beginning of May some students from Nanterre, including Daniel Cohn Bendit, were to be tried in the university courts for 'disruptive behaviour'. A battle between students and fascists loomed. On 2 May, Roche, the Director, closed Nanterre University.

The next day, students from Nanterre gathering peacefully with those of the Sorbonne, were viciously attacked by the hated riot police–the CRS–and hundreds of students were arrested. Lectures at the Sorbonne and the Censier Annexe were suspended. Anger mounted and the University Teachers' Union (SneSUP) called a strike. This was promptly declared illegal by the Education Minister, Alain Peyrefitte.

On Sunday 5 May, students arrested on the previous days' demonstrations were summarily imprisoned and fined. All hell broke loose! Demonstrations were banned and the university strikes spread to the secondary schools. Each application of the iron fist aroused more anger and determination on the part of the students.

On Monday 6 May, a defiant 60,000-strong demonstration in the Latin Quarter of Paris was attacked by the riot police, with a brutality which aroused widespread sympathy for the students among the population of Paris. It aroused, too, the indignation of workers everywhere as news of the atrocities reached them over the radio. To protect themselves, the students began to throw up barricades with anything to hand. This was the first time barricades had appeared on the streets of Paris since 1944, when the workers rose up against the German army before the Allied forces had reached the capital city.

At the end of a night of bloody battles 739 injured were taken to hospital. Many hundreds more were cared for in the homes of Parisians. The middle class were stunned and horrified. In the days that followed numerous eye-witness reports appeared in the French newspapers. One doctor wrote 'with all the bitterness of my powerlessness' to *Le Monde* of what he had just seen from his window:

> I saw, coming out from a cafe, young foreigners bent double, four or five policemen to each, battering them violently on the face whenever possible, otherwise on the shins. The youths had tried to protect themselves with books then the books had gone flying. The blows rained until they were thrown into the police van thirty metres away. How long that short distance seemed! Residents of this bourgeois quarter were shouting their indignation.
>
> One black youth who had been walking normally when he was put in the 'Salad Basket' (Black Maria) emerged fifteen minutes later with his face covered in blood. He staggered and collapsed. They laid him out on a stretcher and took him away. I suppose the colour of his skin had warranted him being 'taken care of' inside the van.
>
> Shortly afterwards in battles with the police the students succeeded in pushing them back–vans and all. Some bottles hurtled down from several storeys up on the forces of law and order. The sympathy of the population

> goes visibly to the students who remain masters of the terrain. Tomorrow there will be police denunciation of 'foreigners' and the real demonstrators will have smashed the cops and I say this with satisfaction...I admit it!

On various occasions when the police were forced back applause burst out on the balconies. No hostility was displayed towards the demonstrators–on the contrary radios, food and refuge were provided. A poll indicated that 80 per cent of the Paris population were behind the students. The government had misjudged and banked on a tiny group of agitators being isolated. Peyrefitte had spoken of 'a handful of troublemakers'. Scandalously the leaders of the 'Communist' Party had echoed these sentiments, suggesting that the movement of the students was the work of grouplets or 'groupuscules'–Trotskyists, anarchists–even OAS and CIA agents!

Young Workers Join In

The events of 6 May led to days of demonstrations, street fighting and the setting up of barricades. As the students' numbers grew and the young workers joined them on the barricades they taunted the government and the Communist Party leaders with shouts of 'we are a groupuscule'. On their growing demonstrations the cries went up: 'Students and workers solidarity', 'Free our comrades!', 'Police out of the Latin Quarter!' and 'Re-open the universities!'. After the revolution of 1848, the Prefect of Police, Haussmann, had ordered the redesigning of Paris with wide boulevards to prevent the city ever again being blockaded by barricades. The very cobblestones with which the boulevards were made, formed ideal building blocks for the barricades of May 1968! Workers lent their expertise and their pneumatic drills to assist with digging up the *pavés* (cobblestones) for the more rapid and effective construction of defences.

On 10 May, on what became known as 'The Night of the Barricades' more than 60 such constructions were thrown up. The police resorted to everything but shooting. Teargas, smoke bombs and even CS gas were used. Residents, at the request of the students, poured water from their houses to relieve the irritation to eyes and skin. The gas had penetrated the Metro (underground system) even causing distress to passengers travelling underneath the Latin Quarter!

In one incident thirty rounds of tear gas were launched into a cafe. Since the first attacks by the riot police students had chanted 'CRS-SS'. In this incident the CRS sought revenge, threatening, 'You'll see if we're the SS!' A first-year philosophy student described how she had been forced back a number of times into the downstairs toilet of this cafe. A number of other women were with her screaming and lying on the floor

Nanterre University. Dumped between motorways and North African shanty towns.

praying! She was overcome by the gas and the hysteria. Half- conscious, she was unaware until she was brought out of the cafe that she had lost the sight of both eyes!

The results of the battles on the Rue Gay Lussac were so horrific that doctors demanded publicly that the police be prosecuted. Police vehicles were reported to have mowed into demonstrators. On one occasion a pedestrian was carried thirty yards on a front bumper and the driver said he hadn't seen him! On the night of 10 May when the CRS stormed the barricades, they would not even allow the Red Cross to move in and pick up the injured.

The previous day Peyrefitte had refused to allow Nanterre to be opened. Generalised anger against the government's brutal response to the students' protests had reached boiling point. The leaders of the major trade union federations and the left parties were compelled to make the call for a 24-hour general strike for Monday, 13 May. Prime Minister Pompidou announced the reopening of the Sorbonne and the withdrawal of the police. But it was too little, too late! The floodgates were open and would not be firmly closed until well into the month of June. De Gaulle's dictum 'the state never retreats' turns to dust! It is the beginning of the end for him.

The government's partial climbdown did not satisfy the students but it was sufficient to encourage millions of workers to follow the students' example–to strike and occupy for their own demands. The workers, especially young workers, were fired by the example of action–the boldness and the *élan* demonstrated by the students engaged in struggle. The students had moved initially over grievances arising from the highly centralised education system but rapidly they began to question the whole structure of society. They acted as a trigger to the movement of the workers. Unfortunately this gave the students the illusion that they were a motor force. In reality the conditions for the workers' movement had already been prepared.

The Boom at Great Cost

THE GREAT STRIKE of May 1968 did not take place against a background of recession or stagnation but in a period when real incomes were rising on average by 5 per cent a year. For some sections of society–skilled workers and professionals in particular–expectations of what the post-war boom meant for them had been rising. In 10 years car ownership had doubled as had the number of washing machines in private homes. Purchases of fridges had trebled. Over one million second homes had been bought. Television ownership was up five-fold.

It was this proletariat, allegedly corrupted and 'embourgeoisified' by the 'consumer society', which carried out the greatest general strike in history. It was this working class which drove might and main to make a revolution. There is thus an apparent contradiction between the rise in living standards of workers, which superficial commentators believed would stabilise capitalism (and thereby de Gaulle) and the eruption of revolution. The upheavals of May-June 1968, confirm the analysis of Marxism that the conditions for revolution are prepared not automatically by either economic slump or an upswing, but by the *change* from one epoch to another.

Economic catastrophe like that of 1929-33 in America can stun and paralyse the proletariat for a period. On the other hand, an increase in production, with a consequent fall in unemployment, can restore the confidence of the working class and prepare the ground for a new explosion of the class struggle.

The post-war economic upswing in France, and particularly under de Gaulle, had healed the wounds of the French working class. The consciousness of the setbacks and defeats of the inter-war and immediate post-war periods, had dissolved with the development of a new and combative generation of workers. Now inflation and unemployment threatened to undermine everything that had been gained. These factors, together with the peculiar character of de Gaulle's bonapartist regime, invested French society with the potential for revolutionary explosions.

Conscious of the dangers of developing a powerful working class in France, with its great traditions of revolution, the French ruling class had, for 150 years until the late 1950s, deliberately held back the development of an industrial economy. France had become known as the 'Banker of the World' and still had a large peasantry to act as a political counterweight to the workers in the cities.

Even in 1968 half the population lived in communities of less than 2000 people. Twenty-eight per cent of the workforce were in manufacturing compared to 35 per cent in Britain and Germany. France's productivity was less than half the average for the rest of Europe. The decline, however, of the proportion of the population of France directly employed on the land, from 35 per cent in 1945 to 17 per cent, was the most rapid of any western country over a 20-year period.

Coming to power in 1958, in the white heat of the unprecedented post-war boom de Gaulle was forced to modernise and to bring France into the world market–in a word: to compete. He was aided by a 15 per cent devaluation of the franc and large scale investment by the United States. A balance of payments deficit was turned into a surplus and a vast reserve was accumulated of $5.25 billion in gold. But beneath the glittering boom the rust had set in. The miracle had been achieved at great cost to the living and working conditions of millions of workers. The rapid expansion had brought with it a 45 per cent inflation over a ten-year period. By 1968 price rises were being exacerbated by new impositions of VAT and deregulation of rents. Unemployment had risen by 70 per cent since 1960 to an official figure of more than 500,000 (according to the unions it was 700,000). A quarter of the jobless were school-leavers, graduates and failed students. Half were estimated to be under 25.

Already inadequate health and social security provisions were to be cut back; in particular a decree further restricting sick pay had flared up as a burning issue. Infant mortality was high for a European country. In Paris, three million people lived in slums, and half the dwellings had no inside toilet facilities.

In industry long hours were worked, often for low pay. A quarter of workers received no more than £12 a week. One-and-a-half million unskilled workers and agricultural labourers were still getting 400 francs per month (£33) or less. Six million people lived below the poverty line. The 40-hour week had been introduced by the Popular Front government of 1936 and widely implemented before the war. Now, in 1968, the average working week was 45 hours.

A Sight Out of Hell

In the giant car factories that had mushroomed during the boom, the most modern vehicles were being produced in archaic conditions. As in America in the 1930s, production lines were policed by private armies of armed thugs. Immigrant labour had been deliberately used in an attempt to divide the workforces. Workers were arranged on the production lines by nationality so that one worker was hardly ever next to another who spoke the same language.

Three million had been drawn from poverty conditions in Southern Europe, North Africa and the Caribbean into the workplaces of France. One-third of the 40,000 workers in Citröen's Paris plants were immigrants. Thousands more, particularly Spanish and Portuguese, were employed in the big engineering firms. Their dreams were shattered as they found themselves living and working in atrocious 'third world' conditions. If they began to kick back in industry and proved too militant, their companies would simply get the police to remove their work permits. Many were herded into hostels where overcrowded and insanitary conditions were accompanied by draconian discipline–no visits, no newspapers, even no speaking at the meal table. A *Militant* reporter in France, May 1968, recounts the situation in Simca:

> The factory has a police state in miniature with factory police, many of whom operate in secret ready to get any trade unionist the sack. They did not only pursue their duties of repression in the factory itself but also in the company housing and hospitals. Sixty per cent of the labour force were immigrants. During the strike, 4000 of these workers had been kept prisoner in a company hostel. Anyone attempting to leave was told that there was no work and therefore was under suspicion.

At the Renault Flins factory a high proportion of immigrant workers were on the picket from the beginning. On the great demonstration of 13 May in Paris groups of Portuguese workers chanted 'de Gaulle, Franco, Salazar–murderers.' A 'Maghrebian Action Committee' issued a leaflet urging North African workers to support the strike and denouncing the dictatorships in Tunisia, Algeria and Morocco, where students, teachers and school pupils were already in rebellion.

The Economist described the assembly line and foundry at Renault's giant Billancourt factory as a 'sight out of hell'. The workers who came out on strike were rebelling against 'les cadences'–the inhuman rhythm of work–the strain and stress, the wear and tear, on muscles and nerves and limbs.

These conditions explain how France could explode like a powder keg. They are the reason for the exhilaration and elation felt by workers once the possibility opened up of transforming their daily lives. They explain, too, the bitterness and desire for revenge that showed itself in some of the slogans and in the effigies representing capitalism swinging from makeshift gallows outside the factories. It explains the occupations, the discussions, the singing of revolutionary songs and the festive atmosphere which accompanied the stoppage of work. It also explains the incidents of managers being locked up in their offices and fed from buckets lowered through the skylight!

There had been many seismic tremors in the years preceding May '68, which warned of an impending earthquake. But none could indicate the fantastic scale of the explosion, once the lid of Gaullist society had been lifted.

The forcing house of the rapid French industrialisation had done exactly what Marx and Engels had predicted in the *Communist Manifesto* and what the French ruling class had feared for so long. They had brought workers together in large concentrations with 30,000 at the Renault Billancourt works alone. They were creating their own gravediggers–foremost amongst them, the youth.

Education Factories

One-third of the French population was under the age of twenty in May 1968. Well over 500,000 of them were at university (in 1946 there had been only 123,000 and in 1961 202,000). At Nanterre, intended by the Ministry of Education as a blueprint for the universities of the future, 2300 students were admitted in 1964. By 1968 the figure was six times this number! An austere composition of glass and steel cubes, it was built rapidly to take pressure off what was called the 'teeming ant-heap of the Latin Quarter' by Seale and McConville in their book *French Revolution, 1968*. Dumped in a suburb amongst motorway construction and North African shanty towns, Nanterre became a 'blueprint for revolution'. It was the birthplace of Daniel Cohn Bendit's 'March 22nd' movement. This was a rather amorphous but quite courageous grouping of anarchists who had occupied offices at Nanterre University on that date in protest at the way anti-Vietnam war protesters had been treated.

Ninety per cent of French students were still sons and daughters of the bourgeois and petty bourgeois. Even ministers' offspring were involved in the May events as were those of the Chief of Police! Crowding these 'gilded youth' into inefficient and squalid 'factories of education', that maintained a rigid approach to education and to social life on the campus, led inevitably to a breakdown in student-teacher relationships. There was a widespread belief that police spies were operating extensively on the campuses with the connivance of the university authorities. Libraries and laboratories were overflowing, lecture theatres overcrowded and three-quarters of students did not make it to the end of their courses. At least half of French students then, as now, could only survive by taking paid work in order to live, which in turn added unbearable strains on their ability to study.

Alain Peyrefitte, the ill-fated Minister of Education at the time of the

May events, had commented in 1967: 'It is as though we organised a shipwreck in order to pick out the best swimmers.' Spending on education had increased six-fold in the previous fifteen years but this was insufficient to provide the buildings and the staff to cope with the enormous increase in the number of students. Alain Touraine, a sociologist at Nanterre, noted that:

> The big new twentieth century student campus isolates students in the way workers are isolated in American company towns. The student crowd is born as dense and faceless as an industrial proletariat with its own grievances, its own leaders and its growing sense of its own power.

French universities have been likened to factories in Russia, working to norms ordained by the centre. All 23 universities in the country were state-run, on rigidly standardised lines, like a government department. Dissatisfactions, instead of being eroded by negotiation and practical reform, were repressed then erupted in explosions of collective anger. Revolts had broken out at Nanterre against rules forbidding students to visit those of the opposite sex in their living quarters!

Grievances about the way that teaching was run and, indeed, its very purpose in capitalist society, were building up to boiling point. New proposals aiming at adapting education to meet the needs of employers made things worse!

At the same time students in the secondary schools (lycées) had been radicalised through widespread agitation and their own indignation at the war in Vietnam. They had been involved, with the leadership of the Lycée Committees of Action, in 24-hour stoppages and demonstrations. Now, proposals were coming through to end the open-door policy of university entrance, to add to the burning anger they already had against the 'Baccalauréat' secondary school exam system. They were only too ready to pour onto the streets when 'les enragés' (the 'enraged') of the universities came in to open confrontation with the forces of the state.

By the time of the May struggles, university lecturers were largely at one with the students in their demands for reform. But lycée teachers at first attempted to hold the 13-and 14-year olds in their schools by locking the class-room doors! Within days they too were joining in the demonstrations and organising the occupations of the lycées along with the parents!

Leon Trotsky, the great Russian revolutionary, commented that the wind of the revolution blows the tops of the trees first–the sons and daughters of the ruling class, the apparently pampered student layers of society. He pointed out that for the first and probably only time in their lives, students are freed from some of the constraints of bourgeois society. University is an interval between the restrictions of life in the bourgeois and petty-bourgeois home, and reintegration into comfortable jobs and positions in bourgeois society. Moreover they are encouraged to experiment with ideas, even socialist and quasi-Marxist notions, which are normally entirely foreign to the bourgeois.

A mass movement of the working class can exercise a powerful ideological effect on the outlook of the students. If a strong pole of attraction develops, the best of the students can be won to the ideas of socialism and Marxism. They can, however, only prove to be sound participants in the workers' movement by breaking ideologically, and in terms of their life style, from their petty-bourgeois and bourgeois backgrounds.

The tragedy in France was that no organisation existed that could assist this process. On the contrary, ultra-left sects, claiming to be 'Trotskyists', reinforced the haughty prejudices of many of the students, allotting to them the role of 'leaders' in this struggle. The revolution was to proceed, they said, under the conductor's baton of the students. One of the sects, the JCR, went to the lengths of producing a leaflet with a quote from Lenin about the working class not going beyond trade union consciousness. The implication was that it must be left to the students to occupy the position of 'revolutionary generals', while the working class merely provided the foot soldiers! This they maintained at a time when the multi-million French workers began to display tremendous powers of improvisation, initiative and daring! Those workers who read the leaflets merely shrugged their shoulders in incomprehension and turned back to serious business.

The Economist (22 May) explained less scientifically one of the processes at work in the early days of May, 1968:

> Obviously many of today's rebels would be absorbed tomorrow and be concerned only with climbing into the establishment or getting their slice of affluence. But they are still young enough to listen with sympathy to slogans about the overthrow of established society. The truncheon did the rest!

The 'Force de Frappe' as this same article had called it– the 'strike force' of the Garde Mobile and the CRS–was a formidable educator: 'France has the troops needed for a civil war and its various regimes have often used them ruthlessly.'

State Repression

The Republican Security Companies (CRS) are an armed security police force created at the end of the Second World War. They were 'blooded' in 1947 when they were sent by the Social Democratic Minister of the

Interior, Jules Moch, against striking miners. They had been called in many times to put down strikes since then and used against all kinds of demonstrations. Never before, however, had they been used so extensively against students.

The Paris police itself was infested with reactionary anti-communists. It was full of elements who hated those they held responsible for 'selling out' France and its colonies–intellectuals and 'progressives', communist and trade union militants. A virulent racialism had been demonstrated against the Indo-Chinese and later the Algerians. This had culminated in the bloody repression of demonstrations of Algerians in Paris and 'rat-hunts' in the streets and the shanty towns on the outskirts of the city. No less violent was the behaviour of the police to those French people who wanted Algerian independence and fought for it. The repression of the anti-OAS demonstration on 8 February, 1962 left eight dead at the Charonne Metro station.

Secret 'committees for public safety' had been set up in the Paris Prefecture at the time of de Gaulle's *coup d'état* of 1958. Elements of the Civic Action Service (SAC), another semi-independent para-military organisation set up by the Gaullist Party, notably including Pasqua (Chirac's hated Minister of the Interior in later years), came into its own during the street fighting. They demanded helmets and clubs in order to go into the attack against the barricades at the side of the police. Others organised some of the police into groups called the 'uncontrollables' who declared their readiness to act, even outside the orders of their own police chiefs. Later, when the Committees for the Defence of the Republic were mobilised after de Gaulle's speech on 30 May, the SAC distributed amongst the police and the CRS a leaflet calling on them to join the SAC.

These groupings were no doubt the prime perpetrators of the worst excesses of the May days in Paris in 1968. Grimaud, the Prefect of Police, warned all policemen against those 'admittedly few among you who, by their ill-considered actions, had given credence to this uncomplimentary image that people are trying to impose on us!'. Elite forces normally isolated from public opinion are nevertheless a brittle weapon in the arsenal of a bonapartist state. Flexibility and responsiveness are not the watchwords of a military-police dictatorship, however tied to parliamentary forms that of de Gaulle had become.

Much of the anger and bitterness that had accumulated in French society stemmed from the treatment meted out to nearly every layer in society by the repressive state machine. The behaviour of the government, the Gaullist habit of ignoring crises, even the barrack-room language of de Gaulle, had brought to a head the resentments born of long years of arbitrary 'Personal Power'.

De Gaulle had commented privately on 7 May about the need for the modernisation of education, but also of the impossibility of tolerating violence on the streets: 'that has never been the method of dialogue'. Few believed that de Gaulle had ever conducted a dialogue with the people–even when adopting the favourite bonapartist ploy of carrying out a referendum.

The forces of the law were beyond the law to some extent. The debates in parliament had little to do with what was implemented by the state, often through decrees. Rigid censorship of the press, radio and television meant little or no criticism could be voiced publicly. At daily meetings of a committee at the State Radio and Television (ORTF) headquarters, the director would have to outline all scheduled news and future programmes to representatives of government departments who then 'suggested' revisions, additions or deletions.

Government control of radio was not as great as that of television. No student or teacher representative was allowed to put their case before the cameras, and film of the bloody street battles was suppressed and only eventually screened when the unions insisted. The round-the-clock French Home Service *France-Inter*, however, broke down the barriers during the troubles. Its coverage in the Latin Quarter was on a par with the 'front-line' reporting of the two commercial stations *Radio Luxembourg* and *Europe No 1*.

For a working class catching up with its European counterparts, and a middle class looking to the fruits of the rapid expansion of the economy, the language of the boot and the methods of the dictator were becoming intolerable.

The satirical paper *Le Canard Enchainé* commented on the stifling atmosphere. The whole of France, it said, was living under 'un cours magistral' (legal proceedings). When Pompidou announced at one stage that he had 'liberated' the arrested students, *Le Canard* depicted him as 'judging and unjudging' (arresting and releasing) students in a totally arbitrary manner.

Ill-equipped to maintain total peace, the bonapartist regime was even less equipped to deal with the crisis. De Gaulle's crude response to the students' demands of 'Reform: yes! but mess-in-the-bed: no!' was thrown back at him with a vengeance in the shouts of the demonstrators and on the posters of the students: 'The mess-in-the-bed: it's him!'

The *Evening Standard* declared: 'The government is acting in a void which comes of years of over-confidence and detachment from currents of opinion and grievances. It is unable to plan any coherent action.' It had stirred up a hornets' nest for itself and would end up mortally wounded!

Storm Clouds Gather

DEEP RESENTMENT at the indignities and impositions of Gaullist rule flared into anger in the 'May Days'. It was matched by a seething discontent in the workplaces of France, which had broken out in significant battles. The warning signs of the greatest general strike in history had already shown themselves in the preceding months and years.

In 1963 a two-and-a-half months' long miners' strike had been at least a partial victory for the workers and a psychological setback for the government. The Presidential election of December, 1965 had seen François Mitterrand forcing de Gaulle into a run-off in the second round.

In 1967, and the early months of 1968, there had been strikes and lock-outs involving engineers, car workers, steel and shipbuilding workers, as well as the public sector. The main trade union federations had called one-day and even one-hour strikes. Although the majority of workers–about 80 per cent– were not organised in unions, this did not prevent them from joining in industrial action, but they were often left to their own devices in bitter battles with the forces of the state.

In June 1967 Peugeot called in riot police against strikers and two were killed. Trade union militants attempting to organise had been victimised. A long-running struggle had been taking place at the Rhodiaceta synthetic fibres factory in Lyons. In summer 1967, 14,000 workers there had been involved in a 23-day strike. Lock-outs and sackings ensued later that year and mass demonstrations were still taking place way into 1968. A no less violent confrontation had taken place at Saviem trucks in Caen. For a matter of days in January 1968 battles with the police had raged not only on the picket line but through the streets of the town.

At the Renault Billancourt plant there was a generally high level of organisation and the Communist Party-led union, the CGT, had three-quarters of the workforce of 30,000 (22,000 hourly paid). There had been no fewer than 80 cases of trade union action there between the beginning of March 1968 and early May over demands for higher wages, shorter hours and better conditions.

Even in the early days of May itself there was no dearth of industrial struggles. May Day had seen 100,000 on the streets of Paris. Young people had been shouting 'Jobs for youth!' with clenched fists in the air. A wide cross-section of workers were involved. Demands for a 40-hour week, trade union rights and repeal of the social security decrees were widespread. The largest trade union federation, the CGT, and the second biggest, the CFDT (ex-Catholic), had already announced plans for a day of action for 15 May on social security and unemployment. They were also involved in plans for mass demonstrations in the West of France on 8 May.

Le Monde (3 May) commented on a 'tense situation' in the Sud Aviation aircraft factory in Nantes, Loire Atlantique. Workers were fighting against a loss of wages which the bosses insisted should accompany the reduction of the working week to 46.5 hours. They were stopping work and downing tools several times a day throughout the first week of May, and the white-collar workers appealed to the management to accede to the workers' claims. This factory was to become the crucible of the great strike.

On 3 May print workers were also threatening strike action over the transfer of work. A lightning strike of bus workers in Paris over the lengthening of hours had meant only ten buses out of 180 running in one of the Paris suburbs.

On 5 May, 560 workers walked out of a sugar refinery. On the sixth, taxi drivers and post office workers were planning strike action. *Le Monde* talks also of a 'crisis in the hospitals'.

The next day, the police trade unions are in the process of formulating demands and proposing action for 1 June. In Corsica young agricultural workers begin an occupation. Air traffic controllers threaten a strike. At the Berliet lorry factory a 24-hour strike takes place over bonus payments. Meteorology workers' unions discuss their claims! Iron ore miners on strike for one month block the Route Nationale (motorway) for an hour. A foundry is occupied, and a clothing factory is taken over by the women workers for one week.

Most dramatic of all in this period leading up to the general strike are the mass demonstrations in the West of France. These involve electricity and transport workers, engineering, building workers, fishermen and post office workers, contingents from schools, clergymen and nuns and above all numerous youth. Shops are shut in solidarity.

The crisis here is that of a severely deprived area with grave problems in agriculture, a gross shortage of industry, and no jobs for youth. Each year 45,000 pupils leave school but even the jobs that used to be available in Paris are already filled. There are falling living standards and a falling agricultural income.

In the opinion of Paul Houee, Director of the Angiers Institute of Economic and Social Sciences: 'The conditions of a pre-revolutionary situation have come together'. Under the slogan 'The West wants to live', 30,000 demonstrated in Brest on 8 May, 20,000 in Quimper, 10,000 in

Rouen, 10,000 in San Brieuc–the biggest demonstration seen there since the Liberation–12,000 in Morlais, 20,000 in Angiers, 20,000 in Nantes and 10,000 in Le Mans. Another time-bomb was ticking away!

A huge head of steam was building up underneath the leaders of the workers' parties and trade unions. More and more young workers were joining the student battles. The behaviour of the authorities–university directors, government ministers and police forces alike–had brought to the surface an anger and indignation that was now bound to explode in every corner of France.

In the Early days...

Many somersaults were turned in many unusual quarters as the students' protests spread to the factories.

In the early days of the student disturbances, Peyrefitte had declared that the demonstrations had nothing in common with those in Berlin or Warsaw–they were in effect just a little 'local difficulty'. By Saturday 11 May his stand against the student demands had been overruled by the Prime Minister, and by the end of the month his career was at an end!

In the early days of the student disturbances, François Mitterrand, President of the Federation of Left Parties, had given lukewarm support saying: 'Even if the students' methods are not the best, still it doesn't mean that those of the Minister of the Interior are good.' By the end of the month he was proposing a ten-person 'Provisional Government', with himself as President, as the only solution to the crisis!

In the early days of the student disturbances, the leaders of the Communist Party and its trade union federation, the CGT, had condemned the students, backed up by the Soviet Union's *Pravda*, declaring that 'leftists', 'anarchists', 'Trotskyists' and 'pseudo-revolutionaries' were preventing students from taking exams! By 11 May they were calling on all workers to take one-day strike action in solidarity with the students under the slogan 'An end to repression', and by the end of the month, power was being handed to them on a plate!

In the early days of the student disturbances, some of the students had gone to the factories to plead with the workers to join their struggle and got short shrift. By the end of the third week in May, ten million workers had followed their example and then, again, in June, the students' organisations and papers had been banned by a Gaullist regime once again back in the saddle!

The enormous pressure from below had forced the leaders of the workers' organisations to do a 180° turn on the question of the stud-

13 May: 24 hour General Strike. One million march in Paris.

ents. Their aim then became to take over the leadership of the movement in order to control it. André Jeanson of the CFDT admitted later: 'For many of the organisers of the demonstrations it marked the end of the events themselves.' The pressure could be released, they hoped, through a 24-hour general strike and after that, life could return to normal! This was a well-worn tactic, particularly of Communist trade union leaders (Georges Marchais, later secretary of the Communist Party, actually opposed even the call for a 24-hour general strike!). It has been perfected in Italy where general strikes of even two minutes' duration are supposed to serve a purpose. The French trade union leaders had often adopted similar policies aimed at dissipating and diminishing the energies of workers whenever they seemed to be shaping up for a fight. Even in the period prior to May they had organised for partial and local movements–24-hour strikes in one industry, in others closures of one plant while others stayed open, or shut-downs of one department for an hour, etc. Often petitions and protests were organised instead of strikes.

But instead of dissipating the movement, the general strike of 13 May 1968 was not going to stop after 24 hours! It was a massive demonstration of working class solidarity. It had a profound effect on the consciousness of the workers. Once they had experienced this feeling of their power, given the underlying social conditions, it would prove impossible to stem the pressure from below. Workers from all walks of life participated in the gigantic demonstrations in Paris (one million), Marseilles (50,000), Toulouse (40,000), Bordeaux (50,000) and Lyons (60,000). The genie would not now be content to stay in the bottle!

In Paris on this day, such was the power of the demonstration, that the police stood aside. The crime rate actually dropped dramatically. There was no looting or window-breaking in the area of the demonstration. The CGT alone had 20,000 highly organised stewards.

One British journalist described the scene in Paris:

> A human tidal wave...no one can really number them. The first of the demonstrators reaches the final dispersal point hours before the last ranks have left the Place de la Republique at seven in the evening...endlessly they filed past. There were whole sections of hospital personnel in white coats, some carrying posters saying, 'Where are the "disappeared ones" from the hospitals? [expressing fears that the injured of the street battles might have been taken into police custody].
>
> Every factory, every major workplace, seemed to be represented. There were numerous groups of railwaymen, postmen, printers, metro personnel, metal workers, airport workers, marketmen, electricians, lawyers, sewer men, bank employees, building workers, glass and chemical workers, waiters, municipal employees, painters and decorators, gas workers, shop girls, insurance clerks, road sweepers, film studio operators, busmen, teachers, workers from the new plastic industries, row upon row of them, the flesh and blood of modern capitalist society, an unending mass, a power that could sweep everything before it if it but decided to do so...
>
> There were banners of every kind: union banners, student banners, political banners, non-political banners...banners of the 'Movement Against Atomic Weapons', banners of 'Parents of Pupils' Committees...Some banners were loudly applauded, such as the one saying 'Let's liberate the news' carried by employees of the radio and television service (ORTF). Some banners indulged in vivid symbolism such as the gruesome one carried by a group of artists depicting human hands, heads and eyes, each with its price tag on display on the hooks and trays of a butcher's shop.

Significantly, given the divisions fostered by their leaders between the different workers' organisations, there were hundreds of joint union banners. Others declared 'Students, Teachers, Workers–Together'. Red flags were everywhere. The *Internationale* broke out in every section of the march. So did chants of 'De Gaulle: resign!' and 'De Gaulle: assassin!'

On the exact anniversary of de Gaulle's accession to power, chants that caught on particularly well were '10 years is enough!'; 'Farewell Charlie!' and 'Happy Anniversary, de Gaulle!' On this giant demonstration workers became conscious of their mighty unstoppable power. Consciousness of this strength is the most important element of actual strength. The dam was about to burst.

Students occupy

Students went from the demonstration to the Sorbonne and the Censier Annexe to occupy, to discuss and to open up the university to workers and anyone interested in round-the-clock discussions on every subject under the sun. The Sorbonne was founded in the thirteenth century and had functioned as the uncompromising censor of books for centuries on behalf of the Catholic establishment. It had at one time been the centre of the persecution of Protestants and unbelievers.

Now there were no holds barred, and a veritable blossoming of unrestricted thought and action was reflected in the posters and slogans that appeared on every spare bit of wall. 'It is Forbidden to Forbid!', 'Creativity, Spontaneity, Life!', 'The future will contain what we put in it now!', 'Workers of all lands; enjoy yourselves!','Imagination has taken power!', 'We will claim nothing; we will ask for nothing; we will take; we will occupy!', 'Everything is possible!' These extravagant, exotic ideas were the overflowing of youthful exuberence, held back for too long by petty restrictions and stultifying centralisation. Due to the isolation of students from the workers' movement, they mistakenly imagined their power came from their own actions instead of from those of the proletariat. Reality was sometimes abandoned and 'democracy' taken to extremes! Discussions were incessant.

The General Assembly of the Sorbonne occupation would meet every night in the amphitheatre bulging at the seams with more than 5000 people present. Everyone could have a say–mostly three minutes maximum but some a little longer. Rooms had been allocated for 'The Occupation Committee', 'The Press Committee', 'The Propaganda Committee', 'The Student-Worker Liaison Committee', committees dealing with foreign students, the action committees of lycée students and committees dealing with the allocation of premises. Numerous 'commissions' were set up to undertake special projects such as compiling a dossier on police atrocities, studying the implications of autonomy on the exam system etc.

The composition of the committees changed, sometimes every day, but somehow things were organised. A canteen was set up in one big hall, a children's crêche in another. A first aid station had been set up and elsewhere dormitories had been organised. Sweeping-up rotas were in operation and detachments of the 'Services d'ordre' were stationed at the university's entrances to guard against attacks, be they from riot police or fascists.

Almost all of France's universities were soon occupied and all sorts of experiments in the 'Critical University' and 'Permanent Contestation' were proceeding apace. Many students showed great courage and resourcefulness–organising teams to construct the barricades, teams to administer to the wounded, teams to carry messages on motor bikes with red flags and so on. But, however proud of themselves they were, however much many of them thought they were 'leading' a revolution, the real drama was now unfolding in a different quarter.

The 'heavy battalions' of the workers in the factories were about to enter the fray and inspire new layers, never before involved in action, to join them. The 'light-cavalry', as Trotsky described the students and intelligentsia, can make the first move. They can create a breach in the enemy's forces, but victory cannot be assured unless the mighty army of the proletariat takes decisive action.

Workers returned home from the giant demonstrations on 13 May considering all the implications of what was happening. In some cases within hours, most within days they would be back on strike and challenging for power in society.

General de Gaulle, President of the Republic had made no public statements and was already beginning to look irrelevant in the unfolding situation. Renowned as a tactician, he nevertheless decided to continue with a planned state visit to Romania as if nothing unusual was happening. Earlier in the month he had described the Soviet Union as a 'pillar of Europe'. He and the Romanian leader Ceaucescu would, no doubt, be huddling together for comfort in the face of storms which could end their respective regimes.

The movement unfolding in Czechoslovakia was threatening to spill over into a political revolution against all the Stalinist bureaucracies of the East. The strike wave in France would threaten not only the existence of capitalism in Europe, but would in turn exacerbate the discontent of workers under Stalinist rule. The general strike was well under way long before de Gaulle was due to return to France.

The Storm Breaks

ON 14 MAY, the morning after the one-day strike, just 200 workers were on strike; by 19 May two million workers were on strike and by 21 May, ten million.

The young metal workers of the Sud Aviation factory happened to be the spark that set off the historic general strike. They had been downing tools for 15 minutes every Tuesday morning in their dispute with management. Now they had been infected by the revolutionary contagion of the students' protests and the sense of enormous power they had felt during the 24-hour strike of the day before. Instead of resuming work this Tuesday they decided to prolong their action and carry the strike to all sections of the factory. They locked up 20 of the management in their offices, and proceeded to play them the *Internationale* over a loudspeaker to get them to learn the words! A guard was put on the door; the bosses even had to have a workers' escort to visit the toilet! The workers formed an action committee and set about spreading the strike.

It was no accident that the strike started here, where sporadic outbursts between management and workers had already occurred. Some of the young workers were influenced by 'Marxist' ideas. But if it hadn't started here, such were the social conditions that had developed in France, it would have broken out somewhere else. Before May 1968–and again later–revolutionary ideas fell like grains of corn on barren land: now they took root.

The students' action and the mass workers' demonstrations had broken the log-jam. Once the movement began, it developed with an irresistible force. On 15 May strikes and occupations spread to Renault car factories, shipyards, hospitals and the Odéon National Theatre.

By 16 May all 60,000 Renault car workers had stopped work and occupied the six plants, in a movement described by the *Sunday Times*:

> In the giant Renault Billancourt works young workers, particularly the skilled craftsmen in the machine shops, were muttering that *if the students could gain concessions from the government the unions ought to be able to do so too*...On Thursday the Renault factories at Cleon and Flins struck. On Friday morning, the production lines at Billancourt stopped too...Significantly the strike began in 'Atelier 70', the tool room. And it was under way before the arrival on Friday morning of a posse of students from the Latin Quarter.

> Inside the vast shed in which the strike meetings of 4000 are held every day, the atmosphere is electric. The only way to describe it is to say it is like an early morning carnival. One banner proclaims 'More university places for workers' children!'...Speeches are interrupted by demands for de Gaulle to resign...The loudspeaker blares the *Internationale* belted out by men of all political complexions–suddenly solidarity becomes something tangible. It is a moving experience.

Renault's gearbox plant at Cléon near Rouen was relatively new and a young workforce had been recruited fresh from the countryside. These workers had not greatly participated on May 13, but seeing what was developing, they were determined to 'make amends at the first opportunity' as one of the workers explained. The Director of the plant refused to receive a delegation so he was locked up and held prisoner. At Renault Flins, 3000 would regularly turn up to picket. From there groups of young workers went out to spread the call to all the small factories around them.

At one Citröen plant, where at most 200 out of 18,000 workers were organised into trade unions, there was hesitation. *Le Canard Enchainé* described how the 'house cops' (factory police) surveyed the scene when trade unionists addressed the workers about strike action. The workers remained uncertain. Then a member of the CGT got a 'house cop' to explain the management's position. 'He was so bad that the workers were completely convinced and voted there and then for strike action!' Prior to the strike, Citröen was known as the 'factory of fear'.

Red flags were hauled up over the factories. At the Orly-Nord airport maintenance plant, an 'Inter-union Strike Committee' met every day and a general meeting was held every morning of up to 3500 workers. Discipline was unquestionable and machinery was even better looked after than in normal conditions! By the sixteenth, the ports of Marseilles and Le Havre were closed and the Trans-European Express had been halted at Valence in the South of France. Newspapers were still being produced but the printers exercised at least some control of what went in. Deliveries were grinding to a halt anyway! Many public services were still running but only with the permission of the strikers.

> At no time did a general strike order go out from the Paris headquarters of the union federations; and yet all over the country a calm, irresistible wave of working class power engulfed the commanding heights of the French economy. In thousands of plants the workers not only struck but locked themselves in with their silent machines, turning the factories into fortified camps. *(French Revolution, 1968)*

The strikes spread to every corner of France. From engineers to transport workers, department stores to bakeries, from textile mills to undertakers, and to the barges on the Seine. Even labour exchanges were occupied and flying the red flag. The circle widened daily, hourly, from the lowliest to the most exalted layers of the population.

The manner in which the movement unfolded in May 1968 bore an uncanny resemblance to the way that the great sit-in strikes greeted the election of the Popular Front government in 1936, described by Trotsky in *Whither France*:

> The movement takes on the character of an epidemic. The contagion spreads from factory to factory, from craft to craft, from district to district. All the layers of the working class seem to be giving echoing answers to a roll call. The metal workers begin–they are the vanguard. But the strength of the movement lies in the fact that just behind the vanguard follows the heavy reserves of the class, including the most backward trades, the rear-guards, completely forgotten on weekdays by Messrs Parliamentarians and trade union leaders.

The leaders of the Communist Party and the CGT recognised that something big was happening around them! In the early hours of the morning on Saturday 11 May they had produced 300,000 copies of a special issue of their paper *L'Humanité*. On the monster demonstration, of 13 May even they could detect 'A great wish for change'! They now tried to impose their own strike committees in the factories. Trying to head off the movement, as commentators unanimously recognised, they had to push aside the newly radicalised and predominantly youthful elements, who were displaying a tremendously imaginative and youthful elements, who were displaying a tremendously imaginative and energetic approach to the struggle.

On 17 May *L'Humanité* unashamedly declared: 'The CGT salutes the workers who have followed our call to occupy'! What call? No such call had been made by the union leaders! They then proceeded to 'warn' workers not to go with the students on the planned demonstration at the state-owned radio and television centre and not to have anything to do with the students' march to the Renault plant at Billancourt. They continued to try their policy of divide and rule and to inoculate workers against the infection of revolutionary ideas. 'The students want to come in and smash up the machines', they told the Renault workers in a desperate attempt to poison them against the students.

With such a large proportion of Renault Billancourt's workers in the CGT, it was little surprise that initially they rejected the students' advances! The leaflet produced by the so-called Trotskyists of the JCR had not helped, and the Communist Party continually tried to maintain a chasm between the workers and students.

The *Canard Enchainé* gave a picture of students, who had not slept for two nights or eaten for two days, almost in tears at being kept out of the giant Renault plant. 'We have come to support your fight!' 'Bravo!...thanks!' 'Clenched fists and the *Internationale* all round but there were still the walls and the iron bars of the gate which stayed firmly locked'. Between 1500 and 2000 students then adopted the 'Jericho tactic' and marched around the walls of the giant factory. This didn't work either! 'The students came back to talk to the workers who sat on the walls and stayed behind the gates once more. But this time, a bit more discussion took place. The workers who were sitting on the walls were mostly youth. When asked "What are you doing lads?" they replied "We are dialoguing"!' 'Monologue' was seen as the watch-word of de Gaulle's bonapartism. 'Dialogue' was now being practised everywhere. Workers got acquainted as well. Immigrant workers in particular commented that they were getting to know their workmates for the first time ever.

Placards at Billancourt declare 'A thousand francs no less; 40 hours, no more' and 'Long live the workers!' At Cléon they include 'Security of Employment' and 'Government of the Left'.

'The Great Tranquil Force'

The political and trade union leaders of the French working class were coming under increasing pressure to pose a political solution. At about this time, Georges Séguy, the General Secretary of the CGT, told Renault workers: 'Any slogan calling for insurrection would change the character of your strike'–a thought-provoking statement indeed! The words of this Communist dignatory were intended to frighten the workers. Instead they fed the intense mood for a political, revolutionary, solution to the crisis.

The Prime Minister Pompidou appealed on the television, in a very similar vein to that of the Communist Party leaders, that students should not follow the agitators and that 'citizens should refuse anarchy'. Far from anarchy reigning in the factories, there was total calm and order.

Pompidou was on his own. Jokes circulated in Paris about de Gaulle heading a 'Government in Exile' in Romania! A spokesperson for the union that covered the CRS riot police had already explained that he would have difficulty preventing his men from going on strike. Georges Séguy, like many a present-day trade union leader, poured cold water on the movement. The CGT is to be seen, he declared, as 'The Great Tranquil Force'! In the midst of revolutionary turmoil, the workers' leaders sang lullabies, while the workers attempted to 'storm heaven' in the immortal phrase of Karl Marx describing the heroic actions of the Paris Communards of 1871.

'Messrs Democrats' and 'Communists'

Marx and Engels wrote extensively about the revolutionary upheavals in France. On numerous occasions, as they explained, the 'Messrs Democrats' at the head of the movement had robbed the masses of victories that they had fought so hard to achieve and opened the way for reaction in a more or less bloody form. The glorious Paris Commune had ended with at least 45,000 Parisians slaughtered, tens of thousands more died in prison or in exile.

In 1968, the annual commemoration of the martyrs of the Paris Commune, on 28 May, now came at the height of a new revolutionary situation in France. The leaders of the workers' movement were once again preparing to rob the heroic French masses of victory. Why did they behave in this way? The answer lies in the history of the Communist Party of France.

The Tours congress of the Socialist Party in 1920 had split between reform and revolution and four-fifths of the delegates declared themselves for the Third (Communist) International. Since then the Communist Party they formed had been the main political organisation of the working class in France. With the rise of Stalinism in Moscow, the French Communist Party faithfully carried out all the dictates of the Kremlin. These were based mainly on maintaining the Soviet bureaucracy in its privileged position and heading off any revolutionary movement that might overthrow capitalism in France. Such an overthrow—leading to a fully democratic, as opposed to bureaucratic, workers' state—would, by example, then have threatened the very survival of the bureaucracy in the Soviet Union.

The Communist Party thus evolved as a second party of reform in France, the agents, partially of Stalinism and partially of the bourgeoisie. Since its formation it had been presented with priceless opportunities for taking power and organising society along socialist lines. Every time, the Communist Party leaders declined the offer.

In May 1968 the odds in favour of the working class were a thousand times more favourable than at the time of the Paris Commune. So great was the feeling that at last the victory was possible that the Communist Party secretary Emile Waldeck-Rochet was carried away by the mood. Usually guided by a bureaucratic approach to politics and seeing himself merely as a leader of an opposition party, he found himself forced to respond to the massive pressure from below with ideas that more truly reflected the revolutionary founding programme of his party. Contradicting his usual stance, he issued a special declaration in which the outline of the correct way forward was sketched:

> To achieve the aspirations of the workers, of the teachers, of the students...the French Communist Party...proposes not only the nationalisation of the big banks but of the great monopoly industrial enterprises which dominate the key sectors of the economy...To begin by the extension of the role of the factory committees and the free activity of the trade unions in the enterprises...it is necessary to end the power of the monopolies and with it the Gaullist power.

Scattered through this and other material produced by the Communist Party in May 1968 are references to the need for 'socialism' but never again posed as concretely as this. Usually it was depicted as a later 'stage' coming after the establishment of 'democracy'. Like their predecessors in the 1930s, the Stalinist leaders of the Communist Party and the CGT continually tried to claim that the situation was 'not revolutionary' and to deny the political nature of the movement.

This was, they maintained, a struggle 'purely' for higher wages and better conditions. But politics is simply concentrated economics. Such a struggle itself cannot be completely successful over any length of time without the socialist transformation of society. Capitalism, in its greed for profit, literally cannot afford to guarantee these demands. A truly revolutionary party would have rallied the striking workers, linking their immediate demands in a transitional manner, to the need to transform society.

Tensions in the Communist Party–one of, if not *the* most rigidly Stalinist Communist Parties of Western Europe–were inevitably reaching breaking point. By the end of the first week in May, Jean-Pierre Vigier, a leading member of the Vietnam Solidarity Campaign was being expelled for 'anti-party attitudes'. Two weeks later, André Barjonet, who was a top economic adviser in the CGT, resigned from his post and from the Communist Party. He was convinced that revolution was possible and that the Communist Party was doing nothing to assist in its birth. On the contrary it was holding back and even attempting to sabotage its development. The main concern of the reformist Communist leaders, exactly like that of Maurice Thorez in the 1930s was 'How to end this strike'. Their dilemma was expressed by his comment that 'We didn't call this strike'. Thirty-two years later, Georgés Séguy says 'We did not call them out so we cannot send them back'!

Power in the Balance

THE LEADERS of all the parties presented the spectacle of utter helplessness in the face of the titanic unfolding of events. The leaders of the workers' organisations, if anything, displayed an even greater paralysis of will, sometimes masked by radical noises, than the leaders of the bourgeois parties.

The communist and socialist leaders perceived their role as merely sounding boards to echo the indignation of the masses, but at no time did they consider that they would be called upon to take over the levers of power and usher in a new society. They had never anticipated that they would have to take hold of the rudder to steer the ship! The *Wall Street Journal* commented that:

> The speeches at the National Assembly seemed strangely irrelevant. François Mitterrand, the opposition leader, and Waldeck-Rochet the head of the Communist Party, were as hopelessly out of touch as Premier Georges Pompidou. They were all part of the establishment, and they were all faced with a popular tide they had cause to fear.

On 19 May, de Gaulle returned early from Romania like a ghost in the dead of night. Twenty years later, in an interview with the *Sunday Times*, the Prefect of the Paris police recollected the night of 19 May. When the President of the Republic returned from Romania he,Grimaud, and the Prime Minister, Pompidou, were summoned and told: 'tonight you will retake the Odéon and the Sorbonne tomorrow morning'. Grimaud pointed out what a blunder it would be. An attempt to retake these buildings during the 'paroxysms of passion the events had reached' would mean that 'blood would flow!'. At this stage he managed to dissuade the President, who from then on remained an impotent prisoner in the Elysée Palace. France was nearly paralysed. Farms and agricultural depots were being occupied. Bank and tax workers had joined the strike. Film-makers had put a stop to the Cannes Film Festival. Horse racing, motor racing and even a golfing championship did not take place. News was partially under the control of the radio and television journalists.

Action Committees

The many hundreds of action committees in factories, offices, universities and neighbourhoods began to link up. In the Loire

Atlantique province, in what was probably the most advanced form of workers' democracy to develop in 1968, the workers, peasants and students jointly decided everything.

In the provincial capital, Nantes, the Central Strike Committee assumed the control of traffic entering and leaving the town. Road blocks erected by transport workers were manned with the assistance of school children. Petrol coupons and travel permits were issued to drivers carrying essential supplies for strikers from the farms in the surrounding areas. So compelling was the movement that the local police and town hall officials stood back, and turned a 'blind eye' to the new arrangements.

A football match was held for the benefit of the strikers. Early on in the factory occupation, an unprovoked and potentially bloody attack by the police had been brought to an end through fraternisation! Working class women took in hand the delivery of food to local shops and opened up retail outlets in schools. Workers and students went out to help farmers bring in the new potatoes:

> By cutting out middle-men, the new revolutionary authorities slashed retail prices: a litre of milk fell from 80 to 50 centimes. A kilo of potatoes from 70 to 12 centimes and carrots from 80 to 50 centimes. The big grocery stores were forced to close. Some small shops were allowed to open, but trade union officials checked the prices every morning.
>
> The unions helped the poorer families of strikers by distributing food chits: one franc's worth of milk for children under three years old, and for children over three, 500 grammes of bread and one franc's worth of other food. Teachers set up nurseries for strikers' children. Workers and peasants, so often at loggerheads, started working together. Power workers made sure there was no break in the electricity current for the milking machines. Normal deliveries to farms of animal feed and petrol were maintained. Peasants came to march on the streets of Nantes, side by side with workers and students.
>
> Thirty-two years earlier in 1936 over 50,000 peasants, mostly employed on great estates had demonstrated in Nantes against the Popular Front government. This was *Chouan* country–scene of the great Royalist peasant revolts [against the revolutionary Jacobin regime] at the close of the eighteenth century. But times had changed. The Place Royale was renamed the Place du Peuple. *(Revolution in France, 1968)*

Thus was demonstrated in action, in the language of real gains for working people, a small indication of what would be possible in a socialist society. In just such a way, nearly 20 years later did the building of houses and the creating of jobs by the socialist Labour council of Liverpool make the same point–more eloquently than any political speech.

In the scales of history such proletarian innovations will weigh far

Capitalism on the gallows. 'On strike. Factory occupied.'

more heavily than avant-garde experiments within the universities. Nevertheless, the workers who were drawn to the universities and the students who were drawn to the factories cemented a productive relationship. At the famous National College of Fine Arts ten thousand posters a day were being produced–in a total of 350 different designs. Numerous leaflets assisted the workers in maintaining their strength.

A leaflet of the Air France occupation declared: 'We refuse to accept a degrading "modernisation" which means we are constantly watched and have to submit to conditions which are harmful to our health, to our nervous systems and an insult to our status as human beings.' Rhone-Poulenc workers declared: 'The action of the students has shown us that only rank and file action could compel the authorities to retreat.' The leaflet for Renault Billancourt:

> The government fears the extension of the movement. It fears the developing unity between workers and students. Pompidou has announced that 'the government will defend the Republic'. The Army and the police are being prepared. De Gaulle will speak on the 24th. Will he send the police to clear the pickets out of strike bound plants? Be prepared! In workshops and faculties, think in terms of self defence.

Workers discussed with the students on the response the leaflets received. The audacity and revolutionary ideas of the students attracted the best of the young workers but they had not met them before. The workers were unsure whether the students would disappear into thin air again, once the experience was over. But they were also questioning what the traditional workers' party, the Communist Party, was doing as the strike wave was developing apace.

This party was planning a Youth Festival of recreation and dancing plus a meeting. On the day that the 40,000 workers of the Citröen factories came out, the Youth Festival was cancelled by the Communist Party bureaucrats. What could have been turned into a mass rally of the youthful shock-troops of the revolution could not proceed 'for fear of infiltration' by the 'enragés', they declared!

'In every cell and in every factory men asked whether the Party was not missing the chance of a lifetime.' *The Economist*'s Paris correspondent noted: 'Pursuing this cautious, moderate, deeply- reasoned policy in May put the Party under great strain. *It is like a man selling stale bread when there is cake on offer.*' *(Our emphasis)*

What a Revolution is Good For

A high degree of politicisation had developed. When well-known radio and television personalities had, through striking, deprived themselves of their own medium they went through France as a travelling circus. But the public seemed less interested in the stars than in the discussions that followed the performances. Less monologue more dialogue was in demand!

New and unexpected layers of the proletariat were affected by the 'epidemic'. In the great strike of 1936, department store workers had refused to wear lipstick and make-up declaring they were 'workers, not actresses'. In 1968 the 'actresses' of the Folies Bergêres demanded to be regarded as workers too! They claimed a wage rise to ten shillings (50 pence) an hour, better washing facilities and a right to collective bargaining. 'We are not all stupid, just because we are strippers', they declared. They played chess, read books, sang songs and held discussion groups.

The famous Galeries Lafayette department store was, as in 1936, once again closed down and occupied. Undertakers and taxi drivers stopped work. The State Lottery draw had to be postponed, as did the Federation Tennis Cup. Footballers went on strike, occupied the headquarters of the Football Federation and demanded 'Football for the footballers!' Engineers occupied the headquarters of the French Employers' Federation. Civil servants, nuclear power workers, weather forecasters, librarians joined the strike...the list is endless! So are the anecdotes!

A foreign visitor was seen going from closed hotel to closed hotel looking for a bed. In desperation he phoned the Prime Minister's residence and got no joy. It was Hussein, King of Jordan! The revolution is no respecter of rank or office!

When de Gaulle was on his state visit to Bucharest he had hoped to give a banquet for Ceaucescu in the French Embassy. But the plane load of 205 kilos of victuals–fine wines, fois gras, etc. never left Paris; the airline workers were on strike! 'Mongeneral' had to resort to local fare. Later, when he wanted to phone the Commander of the troops in Germany, de Gaulle was told that he could not be put through. The operator was on strike. 'But it is for General de Gaulle!' 'And what difference is that to me? I am on strike for the whole world!'

The employees occupying the Plaza Hotel called the shareholders together. They issued an ultimatum to them not to sell out to the British millionaire Charles Forte. The merchant navy came out. 'Even the officers have joined the sit-ins begun by the crews' reported *The Times* (23 May).

Big estates and agricultural depots are occupied. The National Organisation of Young Farmers calls for a general strike on the farms and for 'real economic and social democracy'! In the South of France the markets are controlled by the unions. It is reported that few people in the South are talking about party programmes and rates of pay: they want a *qualitative* rather than a *quantitative* change in their lives.

In the big factories–the fortresses of the revolution–a carnival, holiday atmosphere was taking over. Not the fear of ten years previously but an exhilaration was abroad. The workers of Berliet lorries had changed the letters on their factory to read 'Liberté'. New posters went up in factories everywhere: 'On strike indefinitely', 'We are the power'.

A young worker at the SNECMA Aero Engine factory comments, 'We are fully ourselves, owning ourselves...we feel we are living socialism!' A young worker at Renault says 'What we want is that everything should proceed from the bottom to the top, not like now, from the top to the bottom!'

A *Militant* supporter visiting France was struck by the fact that everywhere people were talking and getting to know each other:

> Everyone was discussing politics. An indication of the mood of the workers was that, as we talked with them outside the big Citröen factory, a bus full of working class women passed by. It slowed down and the women began to sing the *Internationale* with gusto, waving clenched fists. They were applauded by the workers.

School students were seen at the gates of Renault discussing earnestly with the strikers. At times strikers' families joined them in the factories which became bustling 'fairgrounds', as *Observer* journalists remarked. 'For workers this stage of the proceedings was like a deliciously prolonged day off.' And why not?

In Trotsky's *History of the Russian Revolution* he talks of the indignation of a former captain of Russian industry, V Auerbach:

> The revolution was understood by the lower orders as something in the nature of an Easter carnival. Servants, for example, disappeared for whole days, promenaded in red ribbons, took rides in automobiles, came home in the morning only long enough to wash up and again went out for fun.

Middle Class takes Action

When the working class moves in its millions and shows where the real power in society lies, the broadest layers are lifted to their feet. Every grouping at every level in society begins to articulate what it wants out of life. Admittedly in May 1968 petrol station owners going on strike could not think further than higher profits, but even Boy Scouts dared to declare themselves for participation in the running of their movement!

Young banner-bearing Catholics invaded St Severin church in the student quarter and shouted, 'We want to reinvent the church!' Young Jews invaded the Jewish Consistory, issuing a statement decrying the archaic and undemocratic structures of their community institutions. The Archbishop of Paris visited the Latin Quarter during the fighting and wrote afterwards in his Diocesan letter that 'God stands for justice; he is not a conservative. Christians too must challenge the society which neglects the profound aspirations of man.' This looks like the 'Third-world liberation theology' of later years from the very hierarchy of the church in an advanced capitalist country! An *Evening Standard* reporter, travelling by bicycle through the countryside of Northern France, came across three farm workers in a small pub. They were arguing vociferously over the cause of the strike, complaining about the cost of living, the price of petrol, the taxes and so on. Snatches of their conversation reached her:

> What of profits?...Not the workers but the bankers, the capitalists, the middle class...Running off on fancy foreign tours.. He [De Gaulle] goes to Romania and talks about liberty with the students there–what about our liberty?...We have a consumer society–'Buy! Buy! Buy!'...How can the peasant buy with manure?...

The peasant unions are forced to champion their demands and step up their campaign. More depots and estates are taken over! The exodus of 100,000 a year to the cities means a network of bonds exists with the workers in the cities.

In contrast to the movement of the 1930s, this strike of 1968 originated amongst the intellectuals and then spread to workers in every walk of life. This fact, added to the vastly greater power of the proletariat in the France of 1968, meant that every layer of the middle class was not only 'affected' but actively caught up in the movement. They were carried along by the sheer weight of the working class, which gave them the confidence to struggle against the old order, with a real prospect of establishing a new form of society. Every accepted dictum was challenged.

Magistrates organised themselves for strike action but also questioned what role, if any, they would have to play in a future, probably socialist, society! So too did civil servants and lawyers. Astronomers at Meudon Observatory examined the structures of their research centres and found them wanting; 200 museum curators from all over France met to ponder the role of museums in society, while their staffs, feeling 'at one with the great movement of renovation now sweeping the country' conducted an overhaul of the old fashioned, sterile, over-centralised museum administration!

Architects, town planners even statisticians began to feel their wildest dreams could come true and their talents could be used for the benefit of society as a whole rather than for a rich minority. Hospitals run by committees of doctors, patients, medical students, nurses and ancillary workers began to declare themselves autonomous. The medical profession has a reputation for a reactionary outlook, yet now heated debates were taking place on how to do away with the outdated traditions of hierarchy in the hospitals and medical schools and also on how a future health service could really be run in the interests of those it was supposed to serve. Ten thousand employees of the nuclear research centre at Saclay were on strike and raising not only trade union issues but fundamental questions of power and control.

Culture

Just as when rainfalls in desert areas bring a sudden blossoming of weird and wonderful plants, the prospect of revolution began to bring to the surface some weird and wonderful ideas in the realms of art, music and literature. The outlines began to show of how culture could blossom once the shackles of profit-motive capitalism have been broken.

A literary 'commando' of novelists took over the headquarters of the Society of Men of Letters supported by 50 other writers. A general assembly of a newly formed writers' union discussed 'The status of a writer in a socialist society'. A 'States General' meeting of the French cinema–1300 people all told–met regularly and worked out a charter for the renovation of the whole industry. It was too utopian a document to survive: it ran counter to the economic facts of film production in capitalist society. Of course, in a planned economy, nothing of this kind would be utopian.

Directors of provincial theatres and 'Houses of Culture' met for a whole week at the height of the crisis! Artists made a bid for 'socially committed art' and sent their paintings to be hung in the vast 'galleries' of the car and aircraft factories. Actors took their plays to striking factories. All the principal French orchestras went on strike—composers and arrangers as well as instrumentalists. Opera singers demanded more say in what they sang. A programme of reforms in the teaching of music and the arts was drawn up in a marathon debate from mid-May well into June. They aimed to cut across the watertight compartments into which art had been slotted for so long.

The list is endless of the myriad elements drawn into the molecular process of the revolution. There was even more turmoil than before in the schools and universities where it all began. On 10 May a contingent of up to 6,000 from 18 Paris lycées had joined the giant march and ended at the barricades. What the students' appeals for united action had failed to do in a year, experience on the demonstration did in three hours.

Earlier, in February, a meeting of 600 school students had discussed the role of their embryonic organisation but action had been sporadic and restricted to a few schools. Now every layer was affected. No fewer than 300 reports on school reform were drawn up by committees of school children after long and serious discussion with parents, teachers and workers during their occupations.

Even in the universities there had been redoubts of conservatism which had to be won over–the Medical Faculty, the Cité Universitaire (a community of residential hostels for thousands of foreign students), the Institute for Political Studies–noted for its complacency–and also the theological colleges. Some were conquered through political debate, some through sheer infection, others through their experience of physical attack at the hands of the CRS. One of the *carabins*–medical students who had a reputation for being 'political eunuchs'–told a story about a fellow *carabin*:

> He had gone to collect his car on the Boulevard St Michel when a group of CRS fell on him, beat him up and called him a 'filthy student'. A day or two later, when he heard on the radio that fighting had flared up again, he leapt into his car to go and take part. He remembered to take a screwdriver to

dislodge the *pavés* (paving stones). I met him the next morning, he had become an active rebel.

Theological students were particularly rebellious. They described the church as 'An alienating, self-perpetuating society. So much we learnt at the barricades'. The University Chaplaincy organised a mammoth 'talk-in'. A young seminarist who defied the rules of his order to get to Paris for it declared: 'I felt it more important to come to testify here than to go on comparing Genesis l with Psalm 104 as I had been doing for the last week!'

A professor was seen wandering in the Latin Quarter, obviously very upset at something: 'I don't know what is happening to me, but all of a sudden my thesis at the Sorbonne on "The Verbal Joke" in the Middle Ages seems ridiculous to me.'

These academics from the cloistered atmosphere of the universities and bible colleges, had been accustomed to discussing such crucial questions as 'How many angels can dance on the end of a pin'. Now they found the real issues confronting the rest of toiling humanity far more fascinating!

In the heady and unreal atmosphere of the universities there were inevitably some 'excesses'. Few would have approved of the attempts to burn down the Paris Stock Exchange to try and 'knock out the heart of capitalism'. Few would have been so carried away as Ernest Mandel of the PCI, who watched his car burning on a barricade and declared how beautiful was the revolution! Nevertheless it was an unforgettable experience for all, when the strictures of life in capitalist society seemed to be for ever sundered. They had the scent of revolution in their nostrils and it smelt good.

Nor was the contagion of the French revolution confined within the borders of France. Students everywhere were intoxicated, not least in Britain, where a number of protest actions were in train, at Hornsey Art College, and Oxford, Sussex, and Canterbury universities. Students Essex travelling on a ferry from France declared they had liberated the Channel and that 'Paris is coming'!

Students at the London School of Economics, already engaged in a 'sleep-in', decided to visit the dockers of London to organise solidarity action with the French workers. They experienced a rather traditional cockney brush-off! At the same time, the wives of those dockers had been involved in a struggle themselves against massive rent rises. From the council estates of East London they were demonstrating and chanting outside County Hall, Waterloo. When they saw copies of the *Militant* newspaper with the headline THE FRENCH REVOLUTION HAS BEGUN, they shouted with delight, 'That's what we want here!'.

Undoubtedly, the movement in France captured the imagination of millions of workers as well as students in the rest of Europe. A massive general strike movement in Italy was recognised to be a direct result of the example set by the French working class. On 14 November, 1968, 12.5 million struck, building up to 20 million on 5 February 1969. Argentina experienced its 'May Days' exactly one year after the events broke out in France. A general strike movement known as the *Cordobazo* welled up against the dictatorship after initial clashes between a student protest movement and the forces of the state. But how were things to end in the France of '68? For if the general strike ran its full course, not only the French, but the European revolution, would have been well under way.

Revolution or Not?

> All the constitutional weapons which he himself forged to protect his regime in just such a crisis are now so many pieces of paper, even the weapon of the referendum is useless...The strikes have acquired an exclusively political character aimed at overthrowing the regime...in no circumstances will even the most generous offers be accepted (*Evening Standard* 29 May, 1968).

The government narrowly survived a censure motion in the Assembly (parliament) on 22 May by 11 votes, but two Gaullist MPs resigned. Crowds had gathered round television shops and families huddled round radio sets, as in wartime, to hear the Assembly debate. The result was greeted with a mixture of indignation and relief. The transmission itself had only taken place with the permission of the ORTF workers.

Charles de Gaulle, Head of State, seemed to be completely out of touch. He was lampooned and ridiculed. The world's press talked of him as an 'anachronism'. He had stayed away from the situation too long. He had come back and stayed silent. When he finally made his seven-minute 'speech to the nation' on 24 May, it was the victim of a complete television shutdown, and was only broadcast on the radio. He conceded that the people of France might want more say in the running of their lives. But all he had to offer was a referendum about how they could 'participate' and declared that he would stake his future on the outcome. The feeling of anti-climax after that was widespread.

Gaullists began to call for de Gaulle's resignation. The Constitutional Committee was even told to prepare to receive it! His speech had satisfied no-one. Mitterrand makes a call for a general election. A demonstration that night (24 May)ends with workers and students once more on the barricades together.

The policy of mediation and concession had failed to stem the tide of revolt. It had served to strengthen the resolve of the working class to cling to what it had achieved. Sensing this determination–a hardening of the situation–elements in the government had reverted to type. Enough was enough! Orders went out for the barricades to be stormed and another 'Bloody Friday' went down in history. The night of 24 May, 1968, saw the worst violence yet, in a number of cities.

In Paris the situation had been inflamed by a statement from the Minister of Interior at three in the morning, calling on the city to vomit out 'Le Pègre' (criminal scum) alleged to be responsible for the fighting 'We are all scum!' retorted the students and workers. Fierce battles raged inside and outside the Latin Quarter. By the end of the night 800 had been arrested and up to 1500 injured. Two deaths occurred–a policeman in Lyons–and a youth in Paris.

This was the backdrop to a crucial meeting at the Rue de Grenelle. The trade union leaders and the government seemed to be the only ones who wanted the movement to come to an end. The union leaders were desperate for negotiations–just as they had been in 1936, when similar tripartite talks took place at the Hotel de Matignon. The workers' leaders scuttled into talks with representatives of the government which was suspended in mid-air and with representatives of bosses who were locked up in their offices!

A journalist commented that 'Far from overthrowing M. Pompidou they came to parley with him!'–in secret, too! Millions of workers stayed glued to their radios for news of the Rue de Grenelle talks. Scores of journalists camped at the Ministry of Social Affairs where the talks were taking place. Much sought after by the cameramen was Benoît Frachon, the 73 year old President of the CGT who had been a signatory to the Matignon agreement three decades earlier!

On a CGT demonstration the night before young workers had carried placards saying 'Don't give in Séguy', 'Adieu de Gaulle.' 'Power is in the streets', and 'Power for the workers'.

For two days and two nights, 49 'worthies' laboured in the talks and brought forth a list of massive reforms. The trade union leaders emerged tired but smiling. They imagined they could now take credit for something that was not of their making...the biggest benefits secured for the working class of France since the Liberation.

A *Sunday Times* reporter, aware of the balance of forces outside the negotiating room, put the concessions in their proper context: 'any amateur could have negotiated huge concessions in such a situation!'.A revolutionary wave that threatened the whole 'state crockery' could extract reforms from a capitalist class, that years of talking had been unable to achieve. A class facing its own destruction will summon up every last ounce from its reserves to placate the enemy. It will buy time and then devise a way of clawing back what it has given away when the moment of crisis has passed, when the enemy has left the battlefield.

All workers would get at least a 7 per cent rise followed by a 3 per cent rise later in the year. The statutory minimum wage would go up by one third, in agriculture by 56 per cent and some shop assistants would receive a 72 per cent increase. Strikers would receive half their normal wage for the time they had been occupying their factories!

Georges Séguy went proudly to the CGT stronghold of Renault Billancourt. Within minutes he was booed and howled down. Eyewitnesses recount the great workshed packed literally to the roof, with workers sitting on the overhead gantries. Not only did they show their total opposition to the deal. They immediately started up chants for a 'people's government'. To them this could only mean one thing–a 'workers' government'. The Communist trade union leaders suffered exactly the same fate in the very same Renault factory as the Communist advocates of the Matignon agreement in 1936! As then, the same thing followed too. In factory after factory, the offers were rejected outright and workers dug in, waiting for a better alternative to come up.

The trade union leaders had been trying to get talks with the government for two years. Now under the pressure of the revolution they had succeeded and won concessions beyond their wildest dreams. But the workers of France were not satisfied. They wanted more than better wages, better social security and talks on trade union rights! The transformation of their lives was within sight. They would not let go easily of this chance– they had never experienced anything like it before and might never experience anything like it again.

French society is now completely polarised. At this crucial moment the workers' leaders criminally fail to give a lead. The right begin to organise through Committees for the Defence of the Republic and to arm themselves. Yet the workers' leaders are paralysed. On a number of occasions, before this and again after, decisive action could have transformed the situation.

Four Conditions For Revolution

A 'CLASSICAL' revolutionary situation had undoubtedly developed in France. *The Economist* had taken as its yard-stick for deciding whether or not a situation was revolutionary just one criterion: whether a large enough proportion of the population was 'convinced that its conditions of life were intolerable'. Working people live for years, even decades, in intolerable conditions, without feeling they can make a revolution. But as Lenin explained many times, a revolution only occurs when a number of factors coincide, and is successful only when four major conditions are fulfilled.

Firstly, faced with a profound crisis the ruling class is incapable of governing in the old way and begins to split into different wings, each seeking a different solution to the crisis. Secondly, the middle layers are in ferment. Thirdly, the working class seeks a way out, not on the basis of the old society, but of a new order. It moves into battle in a determined fashion. Fourthly, the most crucial condition, is the existence, at the head of the mass workers' movement of a clear Marxist leadership, with the necessary strategy, tactics, and organisation to guarantee victory.

Any objective analysis irrefutably demonstrates that three out of the four of Lenin's conditions existed in France in May-June, 1968. Indeed, never before, either in French history or that of any other country, had these three objective conditions for revolution manifested themselves in such a clear fashion. Only those blinded by reformist cataracts could fail to see what was before their eyes.

Ruling Class Split

The first element of the French revolution of 1968 was the vacillating, the crisis of confidence on the part of the ruling class. The panic of the French bourgeoisie was indicated by the rapid rise in the price of gold and an unprecedented flight of capital. Traffic jams were reported on the roads into Switzerland!

Marx pointed out how, contrary to appearances, a revolution starts from above. Weaknesses and splits at the top, which reflect the subterranean revolt of the masses, are displayed. They in turn encourage the revolutionary forces below to advance. One section wants to use the club to maintain its rule; the other favours concessions. The Gaullist Cabinet was clearly divided into 'hawks' and 'doves' over how to deal with the crisis as it developed. 'Left' Gaullists declared themselves to be 'with the students' and deplored the use of the CRS. The zig-zags from brutal repression to unprecedented concession, and back again showed a complete loss of command over the situation.

Government ministers hit the depths of despair. Christian Fouchet declared: 'If this spreads we are finished!' and Georges Pompidou: 'It's the end of my political career!' Even the most astute bourgeois–and Pompidou must be included amongst them–think in 1968, when tossed violently about on the waves of the revolution, first and foremost of their own personal fortunes. Before the crisis, Finance Minister Michel Debré had been giving at least three interviews and two statements to the public every day. Since the events began he had been completely muted. Then, as if to try and comfort himself, he declared 'Six million on strike? That's not a revolution!' This is known as 'whistling in the dark to keep up your spirits'!

During de Gaulle's absence in Romania, Pompidou had proved more responsive to the pressures from below–'untrammelled', as one commentator put it, 'by the burden of incarnating France'. He then saw de Gaulle making what, from his point of view, must have seemed like blunder after blunder, appearing before everyone's eyes as a tired and bankrupt politician.

The very same voices who now condemned de Gaulle for blunder after blunder, had, in previous periods praised him for being a 'miracle worker'. He had, according to them, furnished the basis for the dazzling economic fireworks of the boom, and in the process, succeeded in cowing the mighty French proletariat. All this they ascribed to his charisma and the powerful weapons at the disposal of bonapartism.

Hegel, the dialectical philosopher, had talked 150 years earlier of how reason becomes unreason. The methods of yesterday which appeared to guarantee success, now, in a changed situation in France, turned into their opposite. The 'strong state' was powerless, in the words of the *Evening Standard*: 'All the constitutional weapons which he himself forged to protect his regime in just such a crisis are now so many pieces of paper, even the weapon of the referendum is useless.' (29 May). De Gaulle, the architect of the strong state was politically paralysed and incapable of taking any initiative. His methods, far from stabilising the situation, had ignited a revolution that they were powerless to control. By the end of the month he was fleeing the country. The memoirs of his Prime Minister bear witness: 'In reality, the general suffered a crisis of morale. Thinking the game was up, he had chosen to retire. Arriving in Baden-Baden, he was ready to stay a long time.'

The Middle Class Won Over

The second condition for a successful revolution is turmoil amongst the middle class. They look to one or other of the two great classes in society–the workers or the capitalists–for a way out of the problems they face. In France of May 1968, there was turmoil indeed, but no vacillating. The great majority of the middle class saw its fate tied up with the success of the workers' movement. That applied to the white-collar workers, the middle management (*cadres*), the technicians. It applied to the peasantry in the countryside as much as to the professionals and the students in the towns.

Theirs was no passive support but active, enthusiastic, direct involvement. New doors were being opened for them. They drew strength and confidence from the enormous power being displayed by the workers on strike. The appetite was increasing with the eating, as Rabelais' Gargantua would say. It seemed as if nothing could stand in their way. Together they would change the world!

'We disagree!' cried the Communists. This picture is contradicted, they claim, by a million-strong demonstration of petty-bourgeois reaction. But that was on 31 May. Two weeks earlier, only 2000 responded to a call by the reactionary para-military organisation 'Occident' to rally against the strike! By the end of the month, the counter revolution had been given the time to pull some of the middle-class dregs of society together. Even so, *The Economist* displayed a better understanding of the real balance of forces in society when it compared the Gaullist demonstration with one of a similar size the night before, organised by the Communist trade union: 'In electoral terms the two big demonstrations carried almost equal weight, but at a time of social upheaval, it was those who could paralyse the economy who carried the most.'

Evidence of the third condition for revolution–the readiness of the working class to go to the end–could not have been more convincing. Writing of previous class struggles in France, Engels had remarked that the magnificent working class of that country had always shown itself prepared for a fight to the finish.

Before the strike started, little more than 2.5 million workers were in the trade unions. Yet 10 million–two-thirds of the total workforce–had stopped work, taken over their workplaces and engaged in permanent discussion about how to run things in the future! Their appetite too was increasing with the eating. What would it be like if they could throw the bosses off their backs? It was not a question any more of just getting rid of de Gaulle and a repressive state machine.

Workers in their millions now sensed the power they held in society.

Everything had stopped. Not a wheel turned or generator operated without their permission. They felt that nothing could stand in their way. In a favourite saying of British workers, 'why be satisfied with cake if you can take over the bakery?' Why put in all this effort now and let go just for some economic reforms when a new way of running society could be established?

This spontaneous movement of May 1968 had welled up from below. The massive one-day general strike called by the left parties and the trade union federations had failed to act as a safety valve, in the way the leaders had hoped it might. Now these 'leaders' had been dragged kicking and screaming behind the movement, trying to apply the brakes! These gentlemen communists, as ever were trying their hardest to appear respectable. The *Observer* pointed to a paradox: 'The Communist unions and Gaullist government that they appear to be challenging are really on the same side of the barricades.'

No other organisation with a mass base was providing a clear lead either. The CFDT trade union federation had been more closely allied to the struggle of students and workers but could only declare itself vaguely for 'democracy', and 'self-management' in industry.

The PSU, a centrist party, under the leadership of Michel Rocard (he would end up on the extreme right of the Socialist Party which was formed later) was sounding revolutionary. Hovering between reform and revolution, its phrases most closely reflected the instinctive aspirations of all involved in the strike. It talked of 'workers' power' and about the situation 'never having been more favourable for the installation of a socialist society'. For this reason, it was gaining ground rapidly amongst both workers and students. But it, too, was incapable of sounding the clear clarion call to action needed to take the revolution forward.

A huge vacuum exists at the top of society. The government is suspended in mid air. All its social reserves have deserted the ruling class. But the fourth condition outlined by Lenin for successful revolution is tragically absent: a mass party with a Marxist programme and a farsighted and audacious leadership, carrying the confidence of a major section of the workers and prepared to go to the end. That was all that was needed; that was all that was missing!

What every worker was searching for was how to forge a socialist society, whether or not they would give it a name. The Communist Party leaders, the only ones in a position to put the pieces of the puzzle together in the form of a concrete programme, abdicated their responsibilities completely. Then, true to past form, they blamed the workers themselves. René Andrieu, editor of the Communist Party paper, *L'Humanité*, excusing his party's policy, declared to the *Morning*

Star (8 June, 1968):

> It is not enough that the main forces of the nation should be in movement–which was the case–it is also necessary for them to be won to the ideas of a socialist revolution. But this was not the case for all the ten million workers on strike– even less so for the middle sections particularly the peasants.

Here is a finished expression of the Communist Party leaders' pedantry and bureaucratic contempt for the masses who refuse to act according to the proscriptions of these leaders. Lenin long ago scorned those scholastics who envisaged that a revolution would consist of two armies lining up, one declaring for 'revolution' the other 'against revolution'. The workers and peasants in Russia wanted bread, land and freedom. They came to understand that this could only be secured through revolution. Moreover, their experiences and the role of Lenin and Trotsky in theoretically articulating the demands of the masses, taught them that only the Bolsheviks could complete the revolution.

The French workers in their great mass wanted better conditions, big increases in wages, the eradication of slums, a decent education for their children, a massive boost in spending on social services, etc. At the same time they had instinctively understood that no matter what short term concessions were extracted from the capitalists, these would be snatched back unless a fundamental transformation of the situation was carried through.

How then did the Communist Party leaders gauge the 'lack' of revolutionary temper of the workers? In a similar situation in 1936 Trotsky lashed the Communist leaders for their cowardice in the face of the magnificent sit-in strikes:

> The scholarly doctors of the Communist International have a thermometer which they place under the tongue of old lady History, and by this means they infallibly determine the revolutionary temperature. But they don't show anyone their thermometer. We submit: the diagnosis of the Comintern is entirely false. The situation is revolutionary, as revolutionary as it can be *granted the non-revolutionary policies of the working class parties*. More exactly, the situation is pre-revolutionary. In order to bring the situation to its full maturity, there must be an immediate, unremitting mobilisation of the masses, under the slogan of the conquest of power in the name of socialism. This is the only way in which the pre-revolutionary situation will be changed into a revolutionary situation.(*Whither France*)

These words would apply with equal or greater force to the Communist Party leaders of 1968. Why did 10 million workers engage in a month-long sit-down strike, evict and eliminate the control of the bosses in the factories? Why did they not restrict themselves to demonstrations, strikes and parades? It is obvious to those whose vision is not impaired by a reformist or Stalinist approach to politics, that the mass of the French working class perceived that only the most extreme measures could ensure the achievement of their demands.

The task of a genuine revolutionary party would have been to articulate this desire for change. Instead the Communist Party leaders acted like a giant brake to the movement. Their attitude was no better than the arrogant attitude of the very 'grouplets' they were so fond of condemning. 'We know what's needed but the workers don't understand' is what this amounts to. They display a deep-seated cynicism towards the very class which *alone* can ensure the victory of socialism.

In the case of the Stalinists at the head of the workers' organisations, their attitude also stems from fear. Once the movement began to make for the socialist goal, these faint-hearts would be swept aside in the stampede! As on many occasions in history, the workers were a thousand times to the left of their leaders and a thousand times more courageous, too. 'Audacity, always audacity and still more audacity!' was the slogan of Danton in the great French Revolution. That should have been precisely the approach of the leaders of this new French Revolution. Instead, they cringed and whined, they crawled before the enemy and cried 'Hush!' to the working class!

Police and Army Waver

A new October revolution, on a far higher plane in industrial France, was more than a real possibility. But it was not to be. 'Impossible!', 'Out of the question!', cried the intrepid Communists at the time and even more vociferously after the events. 'The police and army were too strong!' was their excuse.

What was the true situation? The front page banner headline of the *Evening Standard* of 23 May was 'Paris Police–A strike?' A spokesperson for the police unions had declared that they 'might be compelled to question the orders if they were continually called out to deal with strikers fighting for their rights'. They 'understood perfectly' the motives of the strikers and deplored the fact that they were prevented from taking similar action by law.

There were 60,000 city and municipal police, 14,000 CRS and for real emergencies, a 16,000 strong mobile gendarmerie controlled by the army. As early as 13 May, a police union body representing 80 per cent of uniformed personnel made complaints to the government. They objected to the fact that the Prime Minister had belatedly recognised that the students were in the right and then disavowed the actions of the police force who had been sent in by the government itself. 'The dialogue with the students should have been carried out before these regrettable confrontations took place', they insisted.

A petition was gathering signatures by the score amongst the police, declaring: 'We shall no longer accept the role of clowns!' The branch dealing with intelligence about student activity had been deliberately depriving the government of information about student leaders in support of an expenses claim. Such a discontented and demoralised police force was hardly likely to prove a reliable support for the government.

The total armed personnel available to the state was around 300,000. Even if morale had been high, they were completely unable to do the job of 10 million workers or force them all to work at gunpoint. Moreover, the army consisted largely of conscripts (120,000 out of 168,000 soldiers). Most of them had strikers in their own families and were reluctant to be used as strikebreakers. One soldier, asked by a correspondent of *The Times* if he would fire on students and workers, replied, 'Never! I think their methods may be a bit rough, but I am a worker's son myself.' Only at a later stage, when the movement was receding and becoming fragmented, would it be possible to use armed force to break up workplace occupations.

Neil Ascherson of the *Observer* recalled the fine traditions of the French conscript soldier, in March, 1988:

> I remember how, during the final death throes of French Algeria, when a plethora of murder squads were filling the gutters of Algiers with blood, there arose an organisation called the OCC (Clandestine Conscript Organisation). This was a conspiracy of exasperated young conscripts in the name of common sense. 'End this war', they said, 'and grant Algeria independence or we will use our weapons against the lot of you.'

At the end of May 1968 the aircraft carrier *Clemenceau* was on its way to the French nuclear testing grounds of the Pacific when a mutiny broke out and it was brought back to Toulon. Three families were told that their sons had been 'lost at sea'. A full report of this was printed in the students' union paper, *Action* of 14 June, 1968, but the issue was seized and destroyed by the authorities! The left-wing paper *Nouvel Observateur* reported that after the 5th Army was put on alert for strikebreaking, soldiers' committees were created to turn against their superiors and to sabotage transport and armoured cars. *Le Monde* reported that 'The Ministry of Defence have resisted all attempts to use the army in a way which might involve direct confrontation with the strikers.'

A leaflet was issued by a committee of the 153rd RIMECA (Mechanised Infantry Regiment) stationed near Strasbourg. It put forward demands for equal opportunities for all in relation to military instruction, properly integrated sex education for soldiers and 'dialogue and joint management' (in education) according to the same principles demanded in universities and schools. More dramatically it went on to declare:

> Like all conscripts, we are confined to barracks. We are being prepared to intervene as repressive forces. The workers and youth must know that the soldier of the contingent *will never shoot on workers*. We Action Committees are opposed at all costs to the surrounding of factories by soldiers. Tomorrow or the day after we are expected to surround an armaments factory which 300 workers who work there want to occupy. *We shall fraternise. Soldiers of the contingent, form your committees*!

The full extent of such developments inside the armed forces may never be revealed, but this leaflet alone shows what receptive ground a class appeal on the part of the strikers' organisations would have found. It cannot be stressed enough that a rare situation in history existed–an opportunity for the socialist transformation of society to be carried through peacefully, or relatively peacefully.

'Not so!' cried the editor of *L'Humanité* again: 'Even if the government was crippled, the regular army with its tanks and its planes, was holding itself ready to seize the pretext of the least adventure to drown the workers' movement in blood and instal a military dictatorship.'

Any attempt by de Gaulle's regime to use the regular army, even that stationed the other side of the Rhine, would have had the same effect as the march of the reactionary General Kornilov on Petrograd in August 1917. The workers would have presented a solid wall of resistance. To use the army at that stage would have been to shatter it. A revolution is more than a mere 'adventure'; far greater forces were on the side of the working class than in the opposing camp.

In *Can the Bolsheviks Retain State Power?* written on the eve of the October revolution, in answer to fainthearts in the Bolshevik Party, Lenin exclaims:

> To fear the resistance of the capitalists and yet to call oneself a revolutionary–to wish to be regarded as a revolutionary–isn't that disgraceful?...It (the capitalist class) will repeat the Kornilov revolt...No gentlemen, you will not fool the workers. It will not be a civil war, but a hopeless revolt of a handful of Kornilovites...But when every labourer, every unemployed worker, every cook, every ruined peasant, sees, not from newspapers, but with his (or her) own eyes that the workers' state is not cringeing to wealth, but is helping the poor...that the land is being transferred to the working people and the factories and banks are being placed under the

control of the workers, no capitalist forces, no forces of world finance capital,will vanquish the people's revolution. On the contrary, the socialist revolution will triumph all over the world.

Short of being guaranteed a painless victory in advance, how could the craven Stalinist leaders have found a more favourable situation? The balance of forces was overwhelmingly on the side of the working class. At the height of the strike, when the workers were still advancing, the ruling class was paralysed. The state machine, although not destroyed, was suspended in mid-air. For a critical period, the levers of power were inoperative.

It was far from ruled out, of course, that the capitalist leaders would not resort to bloody military measures against the working class. Throughout history, the French ruling class has been notorious for the ruthless defence of its wealth, power and prestige. But the carrying through of a total transformation of society without violent conflict, when a favourable situation opens up, depends on the leadership of the working class.

The Communist Party leaders wailed about the danger of military reaction. But half-measures, hesitation and inaction are an invitation for the capitalists to launch a bloody reaction. A bold leadership of the working class, basing itself on genuine Marxism and conscious of its historic tasks, would not hold up its hands in horror at the dangers of struggle, but take decisive measures to pre-empt reaction. They would adopt the strategy and tactics necessary to neutralise the state's 'armed bodies of men', mobilising the overwhelming forces of the working class to crush any moves towards counter-revolution.

For two weeks, the leaders of the mass organisations allowed the initiative to slip away from the working class and this historic opportunity was thrown away. The paralysis of de Gaulle in the first three weeks of the crisis shows how near the workers came to a socialist change of society.

A Workers' Democracy?

In the last week of May 1968, a rallying call to the working class to take political power into their hands would have tolled the death knell of capitalism on a world scale. Basing themselves on the programme of Lenin, through their committees, the French workers could have proceeded to construct the most advanced form of democratic workers' rule ever known. To do so they only had to take the simple programme of Lenin, based as it was on the invaluable experience of the Paris Communards.

All committee delegates and officials, at local, regional and national level would be elected and subject to recall at any time. None of them would receive more than the average wage of a skilled worker. There would be no separate, standing army that could be used against the workers, but they would be able to defend and police themselves collectively. A fully democratic system of accounting and control and a drastic shortening of the working week would enable everyone to truly participate in government. 'Every cook could become Prime Minister' as Lenin put it...or every engineer, every telephonist, every bus driver, every nurse.

The workers' action committees could have been welded together in a battle to take industry, distribution, finance and land into public ownership, under their control and management. They would have been transformed from being organs of occupation and struggle into a real parliament and executive of the working people. They could have drawn in the small farmers, small business people and shopkeepers by showing how their debts could be wiped out and new credit made available with no crippling interest payments. They could have argued for a plan to be drawn up for the production of what people need at a price determined by their own representatives. Rent, interest, profit, waste and poverty could have been wiped out. An appeal to the workers of all countries to follow suit would have had a devastating effect on the course of world history.

The pretenders to the title of revolutionary leadership, the Communist Party, proved capable of anything but a revolutionary lead in the situation. This is purely a 'wages struggle', the 'workers are not ready for socialism', they still maintained. But the role of the revolutionary party is precisely to champion even the unspoken wishes of the working class, to inspire and encourage the workers in their millions to bold action behind a clear socialist programme. This, the Communist Party leaders were simply incapable of doing.

On the night of 27 May, the vacuum at the top is most intensely felt. The Rue de Grenelle offers are rejected and workers wait for a lead. The enormously heightened interest in politics shows itself in the massive turnout to a meeting organised by the students' union. The Charléty Stadium is filled to capacity with a massive crowd estimated by some to be as great as 50,000. But the political content is hazy, nebulous, confused. An old left figure, Pierre Mendes-France (a former prime minister) attends. Indicating that he is ready for a call from 'the nation' and that he identifies with the students, he will not commit himself on any programme. He does not speak! No one else even at this meeting has a clear programme to take the movement forward.

Communist Party members had been told to stay away. There were a number of CFDT contingents with their banners, and all the student groupings. Vigier and Barjonet, now exiles from the Communist Party, were rapturously received. But ten times more energy was expended attacking the Communist Party of France (PCF) than in outlining a programme for bringing down the Gaullist-capitalist regime. Another golden opportunity is lost.

The next day, 28 May, the CFDT calls for an intensification of the strike. François Mitterrand makes his call for a 'Provisional Government' and in the process upsets the constitutionalists amongst his potential allies and angers the Communist Party for making no promises of positions for them.

The heat grows for the Communist Party and CGT leaders. They have pinned their hopes on a Common Programme with the Left Federation. They received 9.2 million votes between them at the last election. The Communist Party was desperate to strive to cobble together a Popular Front government. The political representatives of the petty-bourgeois, in the form of the tiny Radical Party, were still part of the Federation of the Left, and could still play the role of a stalking horse for the big bourgeois. Any common programme would include only the lowest commonly acceptable of measures. A Popular Front government would prove totally inadequate to the tasks and would inevitably apply the brakes to the movement of the working class. The PCF leaders are nevertheless forced to pay lip-service to 'putting in first place' the nationalisation of the big monopolies. They rail against governments 'of a type which will not solve problems'! But fundamentally their policies are false.

The CGT leaders now insist they have refused all the way along the line to sign anything in the talks with the government! On the 28 May, the *Morning Star* carried the following incredible statement: 'Some French reports claim that Mr Séguy had been booed at the Renault factory...when in fact the boos were reserved for the Employers' Federation that he mentioned in his speech'! Later on in the same paper they insist that there is no question of Mr Séguy telling workers to go back; he had not called them out, remember! 'There have been false reports that CGT leaders have tried to persuade workers to return to work! In some cases, they have made it clear that they did not consider the offer enough!' Much against the workers' leaders' wishes–whatever their protestations and without their 'permission'–the general strike continued to grow. More and more sections got caught up in the mood of defiance.

The Turning Point

> The working class waits for an initiative on the part of its organisations. When it arrives at the conclusion that its expectations have been false–and this moment is perhaps not so very distant–the process of radicalisation will break off and be transformed into manifestations of discouragement, apathy and isolated explosions of despair. (Trotsky, *Whither France?*)

AMID PRESS speculation about being on the verge of civil war, civil servants ask themselves how power will be transferred to the workers' committees, as they are sure it will! Civil planners and newsagency and publishing house workers join the strike. Gallery owners issue a declaration that 'Art is not marketable!'

It has become obvious that de Gaulle's referendum will not proceed. No printers could be found in France, Belgium or the South of England to print the forms and the Constitutional Committee, incredibly had declared it 'unconstitutional'! This is the equivalent of the Privy Council or the House of Lords in Britain declaring the actions of the government or its legal head–the Monarch–as unconstitutional.

For this body, a not unimportant wing of the French bourgeois, to resort to such open opposition to de Gaulle's plans, the situation must have been considered desperate. Its decision had nothing to do with 'constitutional propriety', but everything to do with the fear of the bourgeois that de Gaulle's plans would boomerang on him and on capitalism as a whole. A rejection of his proposal by the masses would have inflamed the situation, already at fever pitch. Better to wait for an ebb–for the moment, it was necessary to try and negotiate the rapids of the revolution.

The swollen river was indeed in full flood. It had broken its banks. Solidarity action was taking place throughout Europe. There were reports of Italian dockers refusing to unload ships from France as they arrived at Genoa, Leghorn and Civitavecchia. *The Times* spoke of solidarity action by British workers in French firms. Dockers in the Netherlands were refusing to unload ships rerouted from France. Belgian printers refused to print *L'Express*.

There would have been no question of revolutionary France being left isolated. Spanish workers were already battering at the very foundations of General Franco's regime. In Portugal, the dictator, Salazar was on his last legs. An appeal to the workers of the world from a victorious French proletariat would have spelt the end of capitalism.

What was the attitude of the cliques at the head of the deformed

Renault workers reject the offer of May 27.

workers' states? Not until the 5 June did the Soviet bureaucracy take sides. China demagogically accused the Soviet Union of having helped de Gaulle by staying silent! *Observer* journalists commented 'The last thing the Kremlin wants is a revolution in France which would deprive Russia of the considerable support it derives from General de Gaulle's foreign policy.'

But what was at stake was the very future of the ruling bureaucracies in both Moscow and Peking alike. If it developed, the revolutionary movement in France would sweep aside not only capitalism in Europe but also the bureaucratic elites at the head of the Stalinist states.

These considerations must no doubt have influenced the outlook of leading Communist Party members in France, not least Georges Séguy. For his passivity, he came under fire on a radio programme: 'Everywhere the workers are saying they will "Go the whole hog": What does this mean to you?...The statutes of the CGT declare its aim to be the overthrow of capitalism and its replacement by socialism. What about that?' Séguy accepted that this was 'fundamentally' the CGT's objective but...'it remains to be seen whether all the social strata involved in the present movement are ready to go that far.' Once more the leaders decide that the masses are not 'ready', they put their hands across their eyes and maintain that they see no revolutionary situation! By the middle of the last week in May every other commentator could see it, even including Guy Mollet, who had, on behalf of the crisis-torn government in 1958, invited de Gaulle to come back to power.

In declaring that 'the situation has a truly revolutionary character' Mollet was not having to draw any difficult conclusions in terms of his own action. The right-wing of his Socialist Party had been discredited and its influence had waned considerably. But Mollet, with his long experience of French politics, like all serious observers, could not fail to record what was unfolding before his eyes. Only the political myopics who led the French Communist Party still intoned that this was not a revolution they saw before them.

The French economy ground to a halt. A few workers in one or two factories experimented with starting up production under their control, but generally there was a reign of peace throughout industry and society as a whole. The Stock Exchange and the Bank of France had been out of action for some time. Civil servants had set up a committee to supervise the senior officials at the finance ministry. But in the last days of May little was happening on this front either. *The Economist* commented that 'in the extravagant turmoil there was a silence of the powers that be' and 'The employers' organisations are quiet, as are their members'!

By 29 May all the heavy battalions of the working class had declared themselves against any deals–the miners of the North, the Renault workers, the Citröen workers, the aircraft workers, Berliet lorries, Rhodiaceta fibres, Orly and Le Bourget airport workers. This was in spite of the fact that many offers were even above those agreed at the Rue de Grenelle. In Brittany, new strikes of small firms broke out. Caen is cut off by students and workers. Massive concessions had been offered to save capitalism; now even that desperate measure seems to have failed.

The *Evening Standard* commented that, 'The general strike, far from showing signs of ending, is assuming more and more of an insurrectional and openly political character'. Hundreds of action committees in occupied factories are demanding a 'government of the people'.

On the morning of 29 May, a Cabinet meeting was due to take place. It never did! De Gaulle, the incarnation of the state itself, had packed his bags. He commented to the new American Ambassador, Sargent Shriver, that morning: 'As for the future, Mr Ambassador, it depends not on us, it depends on God!' He promptly left Paris by helicopter. Before leaving he is said to have handed to a top servant of the state, the key to a safe in which his political testament was kept. He did not appear at his country house, Colombey, and seemed literally to have disappeared from the face of the earth. In the ensuing few hours he had to calculate whether he could depend on the leaders of the workers' organisations not being forced to challenge for power. Could he summon up the necessary forces to defeat them?

'France has no effective Government', declared the *Evening Standard*. The workers still wait for an initiative from their organisations. A situation existed like that during the French revolution of 1848, described by Engels, when:

> The proletarian masses themselves, even in Paris after the victory, were still absolutely in the dark as to the path to be taken. And yet the movement was there, instinctive, spontaneous, irrepressible. Was not this the situation in which a revolution had to succeed? (Introduction to *Class Struggles in France*)

All that was necessary was a programme for the linking up of the committees and for taking power. An article in the June 1968 issue of *Militant* explained:

> In every shop, factory and workplace the workers' councils would naturally be the dominant form of organisation. Established at local level they would come together in the districts and at national level the organised sections would be drawn in until they embraced all the toilers–the Parliament of the masses–where their will and demands would be exercised; real democracy as opposed to the sham democracy of the jugglers in the National Assembly. Taking up the demands of the workers, the farmers and the middle class, it would be possible to tie them together, feeling the common need for a drastic change, the need for a socialist society. Once in power the workers' councils, where all officials would be elected and subject to recall, from being instruments of struggle for power, would then become the organs of management and control for the masses themselves. This is what the French working classes are groping for, as the strategists of capital so cunningly understand. The only thing that stands between them and extinction are the leaders of the mass organisations.

The Communist Party tops had precisely aimed to prevent the committees from linking up with each other. There was no National Coordinating Committee–no Central Workers' Council–and workers remained isolated.

The *Evening Standard* (31 May) depicted the central committee of the Communist Party as having all the levers of power in its hands, 'and yet they do not want to take power!' it exclaimed. And *The Economist* correspondent in Paris on the same date reports: 'At this very moment, the one vital question in Paris is power–who holds it or who will seize it?' The Communist Party maintained afterwards that 'never for a moment was power vacant'!

That night well over half a million workers demonstrated behind the CGT banners in Paris. Placards declared: 'The Sixth Republic: that's us!', 'People's Government'. The Metro workers had a special message:

'De Gaulle–underground'! The paper of the British Communist Party, the *Morning Star*, maintained that the French Communist Party had 'throughout the present crisis, systematically and single-mindedly fought for the replacement of de Gaulle by a people's government'!' If so, why not move to brush aside the General and his whole rotten system right then? It would be as easy as as a shire-horse swishing away an irritating fly!

Shakespeare wrote, 'There is a tide in the affairs of men, which taken at its flood, leads on to fortune. Omitted, all the voyage of their life is bound in shallows and in miseries.' Again, the moment for action came and went, and the workers' leaders issued no call to move to transform society. Such critical periods cannot last long.

Dual Power

A general strike, even one of such a monumental scale as this one, does not automatically give the power to the working class. It merely poses the question of power before the workers and their organisations. Two states vie for mastery of society. On the one side is the enfeebled bourgeois state reeling from the blows of the revolution. De Gaulle's flight was the most vivid expression of how fragile was the confidence of the bourgeois state. It was similar to the bolt of Kaiser Wilhelm across the Belgian border as the revolution of 1918 engulfed German society. On the other, is the embryo of a new workers' state. This resides in the committees and shows itself in the iron control exercised by the workers over the factories.

But power does not fall into the lap of the working class like some overripe fruit from a tree! It has to be taken. History has shown that a general strike which does not lead to the taking of power is like a demonstration with folded arms. The general strike must be the starting point from which to organise, to coordinate, to ratify what the mass, the working class, had already begun–concrete planning for the establishment of a new workers' state.

The chief role of the revolutionary party in this situation is to imbue the masses with a sense of their own power, to make conscious what was already unconsciously at work in the mind of the masses. Unless a systematic and unswerving plan for the conquest of power is prepared and carried out in good season, an ebb will inevitably set in. The masses lose faith, begin to fall into indifference, and the forces of the counter-revolution begin to raise their heads. If the movement does not go forward to revolution, it will go back, and allow reaction to get the upper hand.

De Gaulle arrived back in Paris on the morning of 30 May. Later in the day he spoke to the nation for four-and-a-half minutes. With a sudden miraculous access of strength he declared that the referendum would be dropped, the Assembly was dissolved, and that a General Election would take place in the third week of June. He launched a red scare. 'The country', he said, 'is threatened with Communist dictatorship.' His favourite 'Me or chaos' line was brought out and dusted off, echoing the traditional cry of the French Bourbon tyrants–'After us the deluge'. He made an open call for 'civil action' through the renamed Republican Committees and threatened the use of 'other means' if and when necessary.

The spool of the revolution was destined to unwind, but even now the question was not yet decided. Feeling their way back to safe ground, all the old reactionary elements in society began to creep out of the woodwork. Up to a million, predominantly old and middle-class, were bussed in from all over the country to march through the streets of Paris on the day of de Gaulle's return:

> Scarcely had the General finished, than his supporters flocked to their own demonstration. The frightened, the frustrated...who had been seething with indignation during the past few weeks were filling the Place de la Concorde, ready to march up the Champs Elysées towards the Arc de Triomphe...probably not so many as the marchers on 13 May, even if the police looking through magnifying glasses for a change spoke in millions...It was the sacred union of all shades of the right. Former collaborators of Vichy marched with veterans of the Free French; men carrying the United States flag walked behind Gaullist ministers and deputies, self-proclaimed fighters against the 'American hegemony'; advocates of colonial liberation marched side by side with *Algérie Francaise* fanatics, and mealy-mouthed liberals with fascist thugs. (Daniel Singer, *Prelude to Revolution*)

With the workers' leaders failing to provide a firm hand at the helm to guide the revolution forward, all the old rubbish was dragged up to the surface. Still this 'Party of Fear' represented very little in society–human dust of a decaying class that would have been swept away by the youthful revolution. Now that the revolutionary tide was ebbing these frenzied petit bourgeois screamed hysterically: 'Communism shall not pass!', 'France for the French', 'Cohn Bendit to Dachau', 'Mitterrand to the stake', amongst other equally vile, chauvinistic slogans.

Lorry loads of soldiers appear just two-and-a-half miles from the centre of Paris. Tanks circulate on the ring roads. Two thousand men under marching orders–two regiments–are reported to be on the move near the French border. Morale has been restored, and orders will be obeyed.

De Gaulle, it became clear, had 'disappeared' to Baden-Baden for talks with the French army chiefs including General Massu, the

Commander of 70,000 French forces in Germany. This was a last resort for the general. He could think only in terms of military manoeuvres and the deployment of troops. 'Like the figure in classical literature who needed to touch ground to regain his strength, he had a need to go back to his roots–which was the army', as his chief of police put it.

The Paris correspondent of the *Evening Standard*, Sam White, revealed later that de Gaulle:

> demanded the army's unconditional loyalty to the regime, and then told Massu that, in the event of a revolution in Paris, the President of the Republic would establish the government on the West bank of the Rhine.
>
> A remarkable feature of the situation was that the only political leaders to receive news of what was cooking in Baden- Baden were the Communists. The French Army, through channels available to itself, let the French Communist leaders know something of de Gaulle's intentions. By nightfall on the 29th it was clear that calm reigned in Paris and that the General could return safely in triumph.

He did a deal with Massu, the 'Butcher of Algiers', buying loyalty in the execution of any task the President might assign. In return, General Raoul Salan, former head of the OAS, the murderous secret army which had been dedicated to keep Algeria French, would be released from prison. (The following month, he and other OAS ringleaders were free men).

The promise of military support had partially restored the morale of General de Gaulle but the military option had undoubtedly been considered as a desperate last roll of the dice, if all else had failed. While de Gaulle may have dreamed of playing the role of a modern Gallifet–the general who crushed the Paris Commune in blood–any attempt to use the army would have resulted in its splitting in his hands.

However, the most decisive factor for de Gaulle was the perfidious role of the leaders of the Communist and Socialist Parties. A serious strategist of capital like de Gaulle, even with his knowledge of the cowardly role of these workers' leaders, could not have envisaged that, with complete power being theirs for the taking, they should, like shrinking violets, demurely decline the offer!

The deputies in the now dissolved Assembly appeared completely confused if not demented. The 'Lefts' decided to sing the *Internationale*–the first time ever in that hallowed hall! But it was a mere gesture–they had no explanation for what had happened and were simply tossed around by events beyond their control.

Within 24 hours de Gaulle had made a comeback. What was the explanation? 'When he declared that the state was still there, the

Farmers join the struggle. Nantes, 24 May.

Communists appeared almost relieved' wrote *The Economist* (1 June, 1968). They could have taken power; it was being thrust into their hands by the mighty workers' movement but they refused to take it. It was they who had allowed de Gaulle to recover the initiative.

For him the burning question of the hour was how to derail the revolution, how to dislodge the workers from the factories. At all costs it was necessary to steer French society out of the stormy seas of the revolution into the calm waters of parliamentary elections. The parliamentary cretins who led the French Communist Party as well as those of the Socialist Party, eagerly embraced this proposal.

De Gaulle now entered the election campaign by getting rid of a number of ministers who had not already resigned, and proceeded to put into effect his virulently anti-communist campaign, raising the bogey of Stalinist dictatorship to stamp on any idea of radical reform. But could he succeed? Would his luck last? Wouldn't he be swept away by the election and a Communist-Socialist government come to power?

The Communist Party eagerly entered the campaign. Instead of making a bid for power, they welcomed the elections as an opportunity for the people to have their say–as if they had not made their wishes absolutely clear already! They gave up a sure victory and set about trying to demobilise the troops. They called on workers to negotiate the best deals possible and return to work even if other sections were staying out.

Communist Alternative?

In their electoral campaign they played down any socialist aspect of their programme. Previously they had been trying to forge agreement with the Left Federation on a Common Programme that would include *progressive* nationalisation–of the banks, finance, arms industry, space, aircraft and air transport, a national investment bank and committees for workers' power and control. When this failed, they entered the campaign looking more moderate even than the socialists. They peddled meaningless phrases like 'Democratic modernisation of economic, social and political structures'. Worst of all, they tried to parade in the clothes of the enemy–patriotism, decency, respectability. With the 'inspiring' slogan: 'Against disorders, against anarchy, vote Communist', they endeavoured to pose as an alternative party of 'law and order' to that of de Gaulle. They adopted the banner of the French bourgeois Republic in preference to the red flag of the international workers' movement. Communists in Britain had even organised a march to the French embassy under the red flag and the tricolour of France!

Instead of arguing for workers' democracy on the basis of nationalisation of the monopolies under democratic workers' control and management as the only way to *guarantee* shorter hours, higher living standards, new homes for workers' families etc., they argued for a 'New democracy that will open the way to socialism'. How long would workers have to wait? Did this mean there were two stages to the socialist transformation or a slow, gradual build up until the capitalists just gave way? Or both?

At the end of 1968, the PCF Central Committee spelled it out:

> The best method of opening the way to socialism in our country is to organise the struggle of the masses against personal power, for an advanced democracy, to weaken the position of large-scale capital in the life of the nation, to bring about such a movement of the people for socialism that the monopolies would be forced to give up their positions without being able to resort to civil war to oppose the popular will.

What illusions in the good will of the capitalist enemy! What muddled, completely non-Marxist thinking!

To be sure of victory in the June 1968 Elections, the Communist Party should have argued for a Communist-Socialist government on a programme to nationalise the firms of the top 200 families. They could have counterposed the 'order' of the planned economy against the 'anarchy' of the capitalist market– socialist democracy as against the

'Cosmopolitan conspiracy of capitalism', as Marx called it. They could have put forward a programme to attract the small farmer, shopkeeper and small business people, including the cancellation of their debts, the provision of cheap credit and aid, which would have rallied these sections behind the banner of the workers' party. Instead they were trying to compete with de Gaulle on his home ground.

The Communist Party of France had failed to recognise one of the most important lessons of the French events. The middle layers in society will be won over by bold action for change on the part of the working class, *not* by moderation and attempts to introduce alien class ideas into the programme of the workers' party.

Election Results

The outcome of the election proved that, when the classes become polarised, as they had so dramatically in the course of the general strike, then the parties most clearly expressing their class interests gain most. The small centrist party, the PSU who had talked of 'workers' power' and described the situation at the end of May as 'never more favourable for installing socialism', doubled its vote from 495,412 in 1967 to 874,212. Due to the vagaries of the French electoral system, it also lost its three deputies.

The Communist Party lost 604,675 votes and half of its deputies (in 1967 they had got 5,039,032 votes). The Left Federation lost a similar number of votes, 570,107, retaining just 57 seats against the previous 118. This represented the worst fall in votes for the socialists in their history. Later in the year the Left Federation broke up and the following year the rump of the SFIO (Socialist Party) could manage only 4 per cent of the vote!

The Gaullists gained almost exactly the number of votes that the Left had lost–1,214,623. How could this happen? The Communist Party claimed that a large number of Gaullists who had not used their vote for 20 years rallied to the general. But there had been ten million strikers and not even all of them had voted for the left parties against de Gaulle! How could they explain that?

Easy! The Communist Parties of the world declared in unison that these results simply 'proved', beyond a shadow of a doubt, that the situation in France had never been revolutionary! The Communists were right not to have tried to make a revolution. Obviously the workers were not ready, otherwise how could they allow de Gaulle such a triumph? Once more they tried to deflect blame from themselves onto the working class. What the elections *had* proved was that the so-called 'revolutionary' party–the Communist Party–had failed to convince

France's 15 million workers, their families and the middle class that socialism could work!

During the strike, all the doubts in workers' minds about whether they could change society had evaporated. If the outcome of the strike had been different, they would have proved to themselves and the world what they were capable of. But once the movement begins to recede, when they have to bend once more to the yoke, those doubts inevitably flood back. Fear of the unknown is exploited by the propaganda of the counter-revolution. Unless it is countered energetically by the propaganda of the revolution, it will have an effect.

The Gaullist electoral system was, of course, heavily biassed against the working class areas of France and especially against the youth. The five million 16-21-year olds in France who had become rapidly politicised had no voice at the election. Even 200,000 who had reached the voting age of 21 in the past three months were excluded because the old lists were used. The millions of immigrants and their families also had no vote. Election material was not circulated in the forces, apart from that of the Gaullists.

The weighting of the constituencies in favour of the rural areas was such that each Communist deputy had to have on average 135,000 votes, whereas the Gaullists only needed 27,000! Nevertheless, only a few months before the May events, the Gaullists had been expected to lose out in forthcoming elections. In spite of the biassed electoral system, after such a wave of unrest, they should have been destined to an ignominious and permanent defeat.

Instead, thanks entirely to the cowardly position taken by the Communist Party, not only Gaullism, but de Gaulle and capitalism itself had recovered–for a period, at least. Up to one million voters, faced with a choice between the 'law and order' claims of the Communists and those of de Gaulle, preferred the devil they knew–the expert. But for de Gaulle personally, his victory was to be a Pyrrhic one.

In July, with the aim of clearing out any possible rivals for his job, he unceremoniously dumped his most faithful servant, Pompidou. He had gained too much popularity to share the same sunlight as this Bonaparte! But within a year, Georges Pompidou, the former Rothschild banking tycoon, was President of the French Republic. General de Gaulle had been dealt a mortal blow by the Great Strike of the workers. The *coup de grâce* was administered by his own hand. He finally called a referendum on participation, regional government, and was defeated. After that, he simply faded from the scene of history. 'Nothing would ever be the same again', the British press commented.'In the long term the elections were merely a side show.'

The Lessons of May '68

THOSE IN whose interests it is to dampen down militancy on the part of workers and youth, point to the experience of 1968 and declare that it is no use fighting: you only end up with reaction strengthened! They cite Marx's comments that the state machine is 'perfected' by revolutions. To some extent, French capitalism was forced to find new ways of maintaining its rule, moving further away from military-police methods. But it was severely shaken by the events of 1968 and will never fully regain its confidence.

Workers, on the other hand, can draw enormous optimism from what happened. In the thick of the events they had caught a glimpse of the future. 'It seemed to have a good chance of working', to coin the phrase of an American journalist when he saw the new soviet power established in Russia in 1917. Scandalously, the leaders of the mighty French workers denied them the possibility of trying out for themselves a government of workers' councils: 'We did not lose our heads', declared Georges Séguy!

James Klugmann writing in the *Morning Star* of 6 June, 1968, tried to provide some 'theoretical' cover for the French Communist Party's betrayal. He pompously declared that 'a revolution is more than a cry of rage'. He quotes Lenin to insist that because state power had not been transferred from one class to another, there had been no revolution in France! 'The old state has been shaped and staffed to serve capitalism', he declares. 'It is necessary to replace it with a state staffed and structured to build socialism'. How? Well, for that you need mass struggle and a revolutionary party:

> In the life of a revolutionary or a revolutionary party there are moments of great decisive political struggle, when the working people move into action and in a few weeks can rapidly change their ideas, and there are long periods of patient preparation, education and organisation. There is the courage of the mass demonstration and the barricade, and there is the courage of the long patient perseverence of winning people to understand the need for and character of revolutionary change in society. Both are needed by a revolutionary party.

But which of these periods was May 1968 in France? Klugmann gives no answer. When it comes to revolution, it is just as great a crime to mistake the last month of pregnancy for the first as it is to mistake the first month for the ninth!

Klugmann then proceeds to quote a long passage from Engels'

introduction to *The Class Struggles in France* by Karl Marx. It deals entirely with the possibility of the German Social Democrats winning a majority in Parliament and not being driven into 'street fighting' on unfavourable terms. Just like Kautsky at the turn of the century, Klugmann leaves out Engels' reference to the fact that the street fight and the barricades will come into their own again in the future. They try to make Engels out to be a milk and water, law-abiding liberal in order to argue against any extra parliamentary activity! This is how reformists of the Communist Party try to justify abandoning the revolutionary for the parliamentary road *just* as victory was in sight.

At the end of May 1968 a new society was in the process of being born. A revolutionary party did not have to organise a violent insurrection. The only 'force' needed in these circumstances was that of forceps applied at the correct moment. The general strike of ten million workers had done the lion's share of the job of transferring power from one class to another. Why throw such an opportunity away and start from scratch in a general election with all the power of the state and the media, back in the hands of the capitalist class?

The Communist Party of France, having vociferously advocated the electoral path, was not even capable of using the election itself in a revolutionary manner to campaign for the socialist transformation of society!

Sectarianism

Elements had come to the fore in the student struggles who *had* seen the situation in France as revolutionary. Amongst them were modern day Blanquists who imagined that a courageous group of revolutionary fighters could substitute themselves for the mass activity of the working class. Many, including Maoists and some who claimed to be Trotskyists, were attracted by the romantic idea of adopting the guerrilla methods of Ché Guevara and Fidel Castro in the cities of Europe! Consequently, they had built up no base in the factories.

In the street battles of May, the youth grouped around Pierre Frank and Ernest Mandel in the JCR displayed considerable courage and organisational flair. But they were forced to conclude what Trotsky had explained decades before, that 'Even the most heroic intelligentsia is nothing without the masses'.

But when they had gone to seek the aid of workers in the factories they went with an arrogant attitude, not with the humility that Lenin and Trotsky always urged. They denounced the Communist Party at every opportunity without patiently explaining the origins of the mistakes of its leadership.

30 May. One million reactionairies rally in Paris.

Such people fail to understand the role of the mass organisations–what it has taken for workers to build them up and what deep loyalty they retain. They look for short cuts–easy alternatives to the process of raising the consciousness of millions of workers. They present the need for revolution and the need for a revolutionary party without understanding that these questions are indissolubly linked to the need to transform the existing organisations of the working class.

When it came to the election campaign, a Marxist grouping would have gained tremendously by aiming all its material towards the ranks of the worker-Communists who had been groping for revolutionary ideas during the strike. They could have urged them to demand that their leaders campaigned on the full socialist programme offered by Waldeck-Rochet at the height of the events. They would have acted as a catalyst in the process of questioning that was going on already and assisted workers, especially the youth, in building the Communist Party into a mass revolutionary force.

The approach of these quasi-Trotskyists arose from incorrect and un-Marxist political perspectives. Occasionally they were correct, as in launching a programme, during the events to link up the action committees and use them as organs for establishing a government of genuine workers' representatives. But they squandered any capital they had built up and lost a unique opportunity to reach wider layers of workers with their ideas when they decided to call for workers to 'vote blank' in the general election.

Lenin had generally recommended the boycott of parliamentary elections only if an alternative form of workers' government was already in existence, the soviets. Unless the workers' movement has the strength and influence actively to mobilise an overwhelming majority against participation in elections, it will founder. These sectarians did not recognise that the moment for the revolutionary transfer of power had passed and that no mass alternative to parliament now existed.

In June, as part of de Gaulle's crack-down, the JCR and PCI were banned along with ten other organisations and newspapers. Their leaders went into hiding and some were briefly arrested. They started up again under new names but still were incapable of assessing the period they were in. They imagined that the hundreds of committees set up during the strike could be maintained indefinitely and form the basis of some form of workers' control in industry and society. But committees of the kind thrown up in the course of big class battles cannot outlive the conditions that created them for any length of time.

At the time of the Great Strike in France much discussion was going on in Britain and elsewhere on the questions of workers' control and participation in industry. Tony Benn was advocating more workers' democracy as Minister of Technology at the time. The issue was even more hotly debated under the impact of the French events themselves.

In 'normal' times, elements of control can be exercised by workers in capitalist industry, through bodies like shop stewards' committees, if only to a very limited extent. Branches of workers' parties in factories and mass meetings in every workplace at the time of an election can play an important role. In France discussions in all the factories and offices that had been occupied during the strike of the major issues at stake in the election would have enormously assisted the candidates of the workers' parties. But the Communist Party tried to convert the action committees into election committees for the Popular Front without any systematic campaign on socialist policies.

They turned their backs on the millions of workers still on strike, leaving them to fend for themselves, and launched headlong into the election campaign. With the possibility of political change through the general strike rapidly receding, negotiations opened up everywhere and the bosses began to regain their confidence. They were nevertheless forced to use both the carrot and the stick to get French industry restarted.

Many workers had not been prepared to contemplate a return to work without cast-iron guarantees on wages, conditions and hours. Many took the opportunity of seeking assurances that full trade union rights would be exercised from now on and also that no-one would be victimised for activity during the strike. Where the workers were most entrenched, the employers were forced to offer even more than before. In some cases they offered full pay for the days lost through strike action!

Electricity workers had been offered a 20 per cent rise and a 40-hour week but still would not settle with the management. Bus and metro workers voted to continue their strike. The second biggest group of workers in the country, 1,400,000 shop workers, waited a few days to see which way things were going to go before making a decision. Miners in Northern France voted in a secret ballot not to accept a 10 per cent offer.

Seeing the resolve of their workforce, a number of companies decided to resort to violence and intimidation. Inevitably, new explosions were provoked–new demonstrations and strikes. A thousand riot police were called in to the Renault, Flins, plant where workers were refusing to hold a secret ballot. Big battles and demonstrations took place. As the CRS pursued demonstrators across fields lashing out with their riot sticks, a school student plunged into the Seine to escape the police and drowned. At Sochaux, too, riot police were called in by management and two car workers were killed in the violent skirmishes.

The response in Paris was a return to barricade fighting. Five police stations were attacked. Cries of 'They have killed our comrades' rent the air. On the night of 10 June some of the worst violence erupted both sides of the Seine. No less than 72 barricades were thrown up. Cars and police coaches were burned and a massive 1500 arrests were made.

The CRS were sent in to retake other workplaces–post offices, railway stations and factories. They were sent in to clear the Odéon Theatre on 14 June and to the Sorbonne on 16 June. The School of Fine Arts was taken over by the police as late as 27 June. In spite of everything, Renault workers still resisted a return to work until 17th June. Citröen workers in all eight factories returned a few days later and Peugeot stayed out until as late as 24 June.

Fascists began sorties and attacks on buildings of the workers' organisations. Election workers were assaulted by thugs and a Young Communist was shot dead while canvassing.

Hundreds of foreign students and immigrants were deported in the aftermath of the great strike. Many militants in the factories were victimised–no less than 925 workers were sacked from Citroen after the election.

The radio and television journalists had come out on a complete stoppage of work quite late on in the proceedings. They had been fighting an impossible battle to try and keep these media at the service of the whole of the working class. When de Gaulle reasserted his control, army technicians were sent in to ensure the transmitters were fully operational. Later 66 of the journalists were sacked and others found their programmes closed down. In an act of international solidarity, Belgian radio journalists collected funds for their sacked colleagues.

Weaknesses through isolation and lack of information made a number of defeats inevitable. A certain amount of demoralisation set in. All this was wholly the responsibility of the trade union federations. Once more, the 'leaders' gave no lead. They urged separate negotiations on a plant by plant basis and made no arrangements to encourage workers to march triumphantly back to normal working.

Having flexed their muscles and breathed the mountain air, workers did not give up the position they had conquered lightly. But, having been defeated in terms of 'who holds the reins in society', there was no alternative for workers but eventually to hand the factories back and accept settlements on wages and conditions.

The giant of French labour had risen to its feet in May of 1968. It had broken every fetter that held it down by sheer muscle power. But to slay the enemy, Capital, a sharp sword was needed with a cutting edge–a revolutionary party with a clear, decisive and incisive leadership.

Bereft of such a weapon this giant would be laid low once more, but not without a Herculean struggle. The enemy moved in using all the weapons at its disposal, including the forces of the state and of the paramilitary organisations like Occident. Worst of all was the role played by the workers' own organisations in assisting the bosses to attach the ropes and drive in the stakes. Many sections of workers kicked valiantly against attempts to secure the shackles. One week after the election was called, more than five million were still on strike. Two weeks later, nearly two million. Even in July, some sections were still holding out.

The Economist had commented that whoever won the election would be faced with grave economic crisis and be forced to allow inflation to take back the wage gains of the workers. On 30 May, the Banque de France was making appeals against support for the franc. They wanted its value to fall to increase the competitiveness of French goods on the world market which would in turn increase prices on the domestic front. The franc reached its lowest level since 1958. Projections of a $400 million deficit were reckoned to be an underestimate. *The Economist* had commented that 'No conceivable redistribution of the national income could satisfy the demands that had been granted even if large sums were diverted to consumption instead of investment, which would mean the healthy growth of the past would come to an end.' The Bonn government and the Brussels EEC Commission were prepared to make allowances for France, limiting its imports and lifting its exports in the interest of saving France from another convulsion. The International Monetary Fund (IMF) made £300 million available. Pompidou had pointed out that every week of the strike lost 2 per cent in annual production; every week of the strike had also meant a loss of 2 per cent in every worker's annual income, but this had seemed a small price to pay for a new future!

One million workers were still on strike when the first round of the election took place at the end of the third week in June. Lycée students were not to return to school even at their normal September starting date. But the CGT even signed a deal accepting 'recovery' working to enable French industry to 'catch up'. The annual increase in productivity soared from 7 per cent to 12 per cent, but prices rocketed too. The general strike had been a victory in terms of the massive reforms but, inevitably, wage rises and extra benefits were undermined by inflation. Many workplace agreements were torn up by vengeful managements.

From the capitalist point of view, the concessions had to be grabbed back. From the workers' point of view, a struggle on the political plane would be necessary.

Turn to Traditional Parties

In one month in 1968 workers learned more than in decades of previous experience. They had experienced a rapid awakening of all sorts of ambitions to develop their talents and abilities. They had undergone a rapid process of politicisation and radicalisation. A much greater interest in politics had been aroused. Looking for a forum for political discussion, workers and youth still turned to their traditional organisations. Workers will test out the organisations their forefathers have sweated to build. They will test out the leadership again and again, with a loyalty that demonstrates a very high resistance level.

Workers turned to the unions and the Communist Party. During the events they had learnt the importance of organisation. Those organisations whose leaders had come to the fore in the events had deep roots in the working class. Workers turned to them in spite of the attempts of the leadership to limit their initiative and retain the apparatus under their control. There was no alternative mass Marxist party.

The workers' organisations were still intact and they grew rapidly in the weeks of May and early June. Given the balance of forces, the bourgeois could not turn to military bonapartist reaction until after a series of decisive defeats for the workers. There was no question of the Gaullist regime moving towards 'fascism' in the circumstances, as both the Communists and some sectarians tried to imply. In any case in the situation where the strike movement was receding and de Gaulle was attempting to restore the status quo through a turn towards elections, a threat was not posed of the use of counter-revolutionary methods. Though suffering a partial defeat, the workers and their organisations were still a powerful force.

The Communist Party grew by 55,000 members in 1968. In the one month of May alone 15,000 new members signed up. Eighty new cells were set up in Paris before the end of May. *L'Humanité* reported 'tens' and 'dozens' of thousands of new members for the CGT. The *Morning Star* put it at 500,000 in the course of that year.

Advanced workers moved into the Communist Party seeing it as a party of revolution and not having fully understood its role in betraying their interests. But the increase in membership of the Communist Party was as nothing compared with the prize that was within their grasp. Not 50,000 new members but millions would have flooded into the Communist Party. During the year of the Russian Revolution the Bolshevik Party increased in size from 8,000 after the February Revolution to 240,000 in October–an increase of thirty-fold. On the other hand, there were considerable expulsions from the Communist Party and the CGT of members who had criticised the leadership. More convulsions and upheavals in the party would undoubtedly follow.

The CFDT doubled its membership–the reward for standing to the left of the Communist trade union federation in the course of the events. They had responded more to the mood amongst the strikers and put forward more radical slogans. Factory elections at Renault Cleon and Michelin significantly showed a marked swing from the CGT to the CFDT. It was these layers who went on to fill out the new Socialist Party when it was set up in 1971.

For the workers of France, the May events had brought both victory and defeat; it was partial victory and partial defeat. Because the workers had retained their strength and demonstrated such determination, huge reforms had been wrung from the bosses and their government, giving an idea of what could be gained through mass action. The capitalists had to pay in the short term with significant economic concessions. But power should have been in the workers' hands. Now it was back in those of the old rulers.

They had to wait yet another thirteen years after the Great Strike before the victory of the Socialist and Communist Parties at the Presidential and Assembly elections. After the blow of defeat in 1968, outside parliament and then in the ensuing election, workers felt dispirited. Doubts returned. Perhaps they hoped for too much? Were their dreams utopian?

Workers are not blocks of wood, but human beings, subject to feelings of elation and disappointment. All the great revolutionary Marxists understood the role of the complex psychological changes in moods of millions of workers in the ebbs and flows of historic events. They showed great sensitivity on this question. These considerations are beyond the comprehension of those who base themselves on simplistic blueprints and caricatures of Marxist strategy and tactics. Those who wrongly claim to be Communists and Trotskyists are equally contemptuous and cynical towards the workers they aspire to represent.

In 1968 the hopes of millions had been aroused–way beyond their normal expectations of life, beyond the day-to-day bread and butter issues. The French workers of 1968 had far more experience and a far higher level of technique and culture at their disposal than the workers who made the revolution in Russia in 1917. Their achievements would have immediately been on an even higher scale. Their own imagination and creative talents would have begun to blossom to a degree as yet unknown in history. In the years following 1968, the Communist and Socialist Parties should have presented a united challenge to the parties of capitalism on a convincing and audacious socialist programme. A process of take-overs and mergers had reduced the French family monopolies to an even smaller number. Nationalisation of the commanding heights and a programme of democratic workers' control and management would have given new inspiration to the working class. The leaders now failed on this score too.

Unable to secure victory at elections in 1973 and 1978 they were responsible for further disappointment and misery to be endured by France's long-suffering working class. When victory came for the workers' parties at last in 1981, with a massive 55 per cent of the votes cast, it was greeted with dancing and singing in the streets. Initially a big programme of reforms was carried through but, failing to break with capitalism, the Mitterrand government went into reverse. Drastic anti-working class counter-reforms followed and 'socialism' was once again discredited. Mitterrand even included in his cabinet such hated figures from the May Days as Grimaud, Prefect of Police and Pierre Dreyfus, Managing Director of Renault!

New 'May 1968s' are only just under the surface in French society. At the time of the recession in France in 1973 a 'work-in' at the Lip watch factory in Besancon had become a *cause célèbre*. Workers everywhere wanted to see the powers-that-be back down, and keep the factory open. When, during the French holiday shut-down, the riot police were sent in to evacuate the factory, it was as if the bell of an alarm clock had sounded, and workers everywhere were roused from their repose. All the major sections of workers involved in the 1968 general strike began to move into action and in just the same order. Protests broke out even in the holiday camps and workers travelled to ministers' country retreats to warn them that France was in danger of grinding to a halt!

In 1986, the youth in the schools, colleges and universities of France moved on to the streets against cuts in education spending. This time the mere threat of the trade unions calling general strike action led to a humiliating retreat on the part of the freshly elected Chirac government of the right. One of the trade union leaders actually called on Chirac privately to remind him of 1968! Similar events in Spain in 1986 and the beginning of 1987 showed how youth, mobilising behind a programme of demands worked out in conjunction with the Marxists, can inspire the older workers into support, active participation and also into struggle on their own behalf. The history of both countries has proved and will prove again and again that European workers have a tremendous will to win against all the odds–to struggle for mastery over their own fate.

Today the weight of the working class in French society is far greater than it was even in 1968. The conditions of life, if anything, are more explosive. A process of de-industrialisation has seen the number of unemployed reach five times the figure of 1968 and has left social deserts in many parts of France. A special crisis exists for immigrant workers and for school-leavers. More combustible material, in terms of anger and discontent, has been accumulated and the workers and youth have gained lessons from recent experience, both on the industrial and political planes. Almost any incident could spark off a new explosion.

Similar movements to 1968 will undoubtedly take place and, in the present world context, be of even more momentous significance. Now, as the economies of the world move further into crisis, there is no country in which huge contradictions and explosive situations have not been developing. Britain, in fact, far from being an exception, could be the nearest to an explosion in the coming period. A new '1968' anywhere would inevitably have enormous international repercussions. It would spread like a prairie fire.

One thing above all was proved by the French events–that new generations will take up new struggles with enthusiasm and energy. The working class of France, the youth in particular, who have fine revolutionary traditions, will move again and again in mighty struggles to transform the society in which they live. They will move to transform and re-transform their organisations into powerful weapons for change. The forces for a revolutionary mass party will come from within the old organisations of the proletariat–the Communist Party, and the Socialist

Party (which now has the greater electoral support). Without the development of a mass party with a Marxist programme and leadership, the French revolution will be stormy, long and protracted.

A period opened up in 1968 similar to the period of ebbs and flows in the Spanish revolution between 1931 and 1937, though even more extended. 'Revolution has a very long breath', as Franz Mehring put it. The best way for workers and youth to prepare for the future is to draw all the possible lessons from the history of previous struggles. In the hothouse of mass struggles of a revolutionary nature, the forces of Marxism can grow very rapidly. With the correct ideas and programme they will be able to go forward with confidence. It will be a privilege to experience and actively participate in the next '1968'.

The French revolution has had its dress rehearsal. Describing the Russian revolution, the German Marxist Rosa Luxemburg talked of feeling 'the wind roar about the ears'. She also wrote: 'We are living in times when everything that happens is worth the trouble'. That will be as true of the last few years of the twentieth century as it was of the first.

In France there will be a true life drama that will not only transform French society and complete the revolution started in May 1968. But it will fulfill the aspirations of French workers, frustrated over two centuries. It will open up a new chapter in world history that could lead directly to the establishment of a harmonious socialist society on a world scale.

When the old mole of the French revolution emerges again, and victory is assured, as Marx wrote in the *Eighteenth Brumaire of Louis Bonaparte*, 'Europe will leap from its seat and excitedly exclaim: "Well burrowed old mole!".'

Clare Doyle, April 1988.

Further reading on France and the class struggle

Whither France. Leon Trotsky £2.50
Writings on France. Leon Trotsky £6.50
Communist Manifesto. Karl Marx and Frederick Engels 45p
The 18th Brumaire of Louis Bonaparte, 1851. Karl Marx 55p
Class Struggles in France 1848-50. Karl Marx 95p
Civil War in France, 1871. Karl Marx 90p
Can the Bolsheviks Retain State Power? VI Lenin 50p
On the Paris Commune. Marx and Engels £2.95
June 1936. Danos £5.95
History of the Paris Commune. Lissagaray £5.95
The Rise of de Gaulle and the Class Struggle in France. Grant 30p
The State–A Warning. Militant 70p

Prices as at April 1988. Please add 25% for postage on orders under £5, 10% on orders £5-£10. Over £10 post free. Please make cheques payable to 'World Socialist Books'. We stock all the classics of Marxism and *Militant* publications. Send for free booklist to: World Socialist Books, 3-13 Hepscott Road, London E9 5HB

'Tony Mulhearn and Peter Taaffe have produced a fascinating self portrait'

(The Independent, 25 January 1988)

528 pages, includes 40 photographs
£6.95 plus 90p postage softback
£14.95 plus £1.20 postage hardback

From Fortress Books, PO Box 141 London E2 ORL